The Portable Leader

The Portable Leader

Identifying the key transferable skills to help you lead in an ever-changing world

John van Maurik

THE McGRAW-HILL COMPANIES

London · New York · St Louis · San Francisco · Auckland
Bogotá · Caracas · Lisbon · Madrid · Mexico
Milan · Montreal · New Delhi · Panama · Paris · San Juan
São Paulo · Singapore · Sydney · Tokyo · Toronto

Published by McGraw-Hill Publishing Company
Shoppenhangers Road, Maidenhead, Berkshire, SL6 2QL, England
Telephone 01628 23432
Fax 01628 770224

British Library Cataloguing in Publication Data
Van Maurik, John
The portable leader
1.Leadership 2.Executive ability
I.Title
658.4'092

ISBN 0077091191

Library of Congress Cataloging-in-Publication Data
Van Maurik, John.
The portable leader / John van Maurik
p. cm.
Includes bibliographical references
ISBN 0–07–709119–1 (pbk. : alk. paper)
1. Leadership. 2. Management. I. Title.
HD57.7.V3653 1997
658.4'092--dc20 96-41889
CIP

McGraw-Hill
A Division of The ***McGraw·Hill*** *Companies*

12345 CUP 99987

Typeset by Ian Kingston Editorial Services, Nottingham
and printed and bound in Great Britain at the University Press, Cambridge.

Printed on permanent paper in compliance with ISO Standard 9706

Contents

Introduction

In the winter of 1994, David Jansen, an American speed skater, set out to participate in his fourth Olympic Games. Despite being hailed as one of the all-time great skaters, medals had eluded him, and this was certain to be his final attempt. This time his willpower, talent and dedication paid off – finally he stood on the victor's podium and held the gold medal aloft. And, of course, the winner is interviewed by the media.

During his interview Jansen made two memorable remarks. First of all he said, 'You don't have to win to be a champion, you just have to give it one hundred per cent'; and later, when asked to comment on the example that he had given to other aspiring athletes, he added, 'Every human being has the opportunity to be a role model'.

A role model?

Most of us use them, or subconsciously need them, even when we have left the influence of our parents far behind. Moreover, in analysing any subject it can be made to live and take on additional meaning through the careful use of examples. Indeed, without this illumination a subject will at best be over-theoretical and, at worst, incomprehensible. This rule applies in all fields of study, but never more so than in subjects that deal with human beings and their behaviour. It is the living example that adds shape, form and substance.

When discussing leadership, the role model becomes the illuminating example. But how good or relevant are the examples of leadership that we hold up to those who wish to learn about this elusive subject, let alone practise it?

I would contend that we over-concentrate on the rich, successful and powerful when seeking role models of leadership. Richard Branson, Anita Roddick, Bill Gates and John Harvey-Jones have become metaphors of successful leadership, and highly over-used metaphors at that. In becoming so over-used, the value of what they have done somehow becomes diminished and the average man or woman in the street is tempted to stop asking what it was about them (or, more relevant, what it was about what they did) that brought them to the pinnacle of power and success.

Furthermore, in being so elevated it is hard for the average person in any type of business, or those aspiring to be a better leader in other walks of life, to empathize with them – they are just too remote, their achievements simply too far removed from the aspirations and achievements of the vast majority. It is the same when we try to look at notable figures from history or politics. The Churchills, the Pattons, the Nelsons, the Thatchers are all extremely remote, both historically and hierarchically, from Mr or Ms Average.

Of course, we can look at the more noticeable personality traits, and the most significant historical actions, of such people and draw some lessons for more humdrum lives. However, more frequently we all ask, 'What's in it for me?'; and, truth be told, the value is limited.

Furthermore, it is a sad fact that those at the top of business are moving even further away from the lives and experiences of those they purport to lead. Salary differentials between top management, middle management and other workers have widened enormously in recent years, while in some cases, due to contractual loopholes, even failure is awarded with gigantic pay-offs.

No, at present the onus of providing clear and meaningful role models of leadership lies on those in the middle. It is up to the thousands of unsung heroes and heroines to provide the examples that will inspire their peers. If leadership is *what leaders do*, then it will be by looking at these people for guiding examples, rather than at those at the top, that the lessons will be found.

It is important to emphasize here that, by looking at the examples given by those in senior to middle-ranking positions, rather than those at the very top, we shall in no way be studying mediocrity. Quite the reverse!

In this book, a number of leaders, both ordinary and extraordinary, will illustrate concepts, talents and activities of leadership. What they all have in common is that they remain ordinary people – the sort of person who might live in your road or whom you might find yourself sitting beside when you travel on business.

The method of illustration will be via the vehicles of interview, commentary and analysis, and it will be up to you, the reader, to seize on those behaviours illustrated that most apply to you and your own situation.

Foreword
Colonel Mark Cook, OBE

What do the following have in common: a British civil servant, an Indian sales manager, an American director of nursing, a former south London schoolgirl who founded and runs a development and training organization in South Africa, the director of cabin crew for Singapore Airlines, and a man who negotiates hostage release? Not a lot, you might think, but, as you read this, you will find that they have all had to master the complicated art of leadership to get to the positions they now hold.

'Are leaders born or made?' is an age-old question. If it is something that you either have or have not got, then there would be little point in reading this book. Some people, it is true, seem to be born leaders, and given the right circumstances go on to display extraordinary powers, sadly not always for good. History is full of people who led their countries to destruction, and I have witnessed this at first-hand in recent years.

But this book is not about these extraordinary leaders, with whom few of us can begin to equate. It is about nine ordinary people in different jobs and in various countries who have worked their way up the ladder to management positions. Whether you live in America, Asia, Europe or India, or whether you are in business, government or a profession, you will be able to empathize with the characters in this book. And, what is more, you will enjoy it and want to turn the page to see how each gets on and *why*. By writing about ordinary people, almost as if they are characters in a novel, John van Maurik makes the subject of leadership – which can be quite dry and stodgy – into something that we can all understand. You will, I guarantee, find yourself thinking about how this all applies to you and your job.

I read the book at a critical stage in my own life, having just left the army after 32 years' service. I was very privileged to have spent most of this time with Gurkha soldiers from Nepal. The bedrock of the extraordinary relationship which has existed between these soldiers – among the proudest and bravest in the world – and their British officers for over 150 years has been based on mutual respect, and this, I believe, applies to leadership in any field.

So many times, as I was reading this book, I found myself saying 'Yes, I agree' or 'Now I understand where I went wrong'. 'Vision' is a word that is repeated so often by all the characters that it must be one of the vital ingredients to be a successful leader in a particular job. In my penultimate appointment in the army I was very conscious (as were my bosses) that I was underperforming, and then I read Chapter 10 and it became crystal-clear why – I did not share the vision of my masters, and therefore lacked the energy and sense of purpose to implement their vision with enthusiasm. What is more, I was useless at organizational politics. These qualities all head the list for the key competencies of a successful leader. I lacked motivation, and a braver man might have confessed to this and asked for a move, but then I would have been labelled a failure! I wonder how many others find themselves in this sort of trap – a job for the job's sake.

It was, therefore, a relief when I was suddenly posted to the Balkans at the start of the war there – a move that was to transform my life. Having witnessed the effect of misguided (evil?) leaders on the children in that troubled land, I left the army to build homes for orphans of war or disaster. Recently, my wife and I started *Hope and Homes for Children*, and I am fortunate now to have such a clear vision for its future growth that I can honestly admit that, in the words of George Bernard Shaw quoted in this book, that 'this is the true joy of life, being used for a purpose, recognized by yourself as a mighty one'. Vision is so important for any leader, and this shines like a beacon throughout this book. But, what if you don't share the vision of your boss? Perhaps that should be the subject of John van Maurik's next book!

Are you a Wise Owl, Crafty Fox, Donkey or Sheep? You must read the book to find out, and you will also recognize clearly to which of these categories your colleagues belong! We all, it seems, belong to one of them, and the question is, can we change our spots? Can a Sheep or a Donkey become a Wise Owl or a Crafty Fox? Can you learn to be a leader? As with any skill, there are some people who are born with natural abilities, but even so they probably work harder at polishing their talents than those who have less. Star musicians, athletes, business people and soldiers do not stay at the top without much hard work, training and analysis of how they are performing. And so it is with leadership. Yes, there are some who seem to have that something special (you might call it 'charisma'). But that does not mean that those of us who are not blessed with this have to remain Sheep all our lives! With study, training and constant self-analysis, all of us can be better leaders. For those who have not thought about it before, this book, which is so well written and enjoyable to read, is a good place to start.

Although there is only one quotation by a great soldier, I am delighted that this is by my own hero and role model, Field Marshall Lord Slim, who said 'Leadership is of the Spirit'. Yes, we can put the required qualities of a leader into neat little boxes and all strive to improve our skills, but there is still a mysterious dimension to leadership that makes it such a fascinating subject.

Colonel Mark Cook
Hope and Homes for Children

CHAPTER 1

Lessons from the unsung heroes An end and a beginning

Leadership is dead... or is it?

There is currently a strong trend of opinion that states that the final years of the 1980s saw the waning of the concept of definitive individual leadership in both political and business life. Increasingly, it seems that if political leaders do not deliver strong leadership they are criticized, and if they do they are blamed. Either way they are sunk!

Time is a great healer, and while many were critical of the style, approach and actions of Ronald Reagan, Margaret Thatcher and others like them, increasingly there is a feeling – a creeping nostalgia – that at least they were characters, that you knew where you were with them.

While we are swift to blame the leaders of that era for being too directive or too authoritarian, we are equally swift to blame their successors for being too indecisive, too influenced by others, too grey!

Is there no middle road to follow, or have 'followers' simply become too sophisticated? Alternatively, do we expect too much? Either way, we successfully place our leaders between the proverbial rock and a hard place. Given the current state of opinion polls on both sides of the Atlantic (or anywhere else for that matter), few seem able to overcome that particular dilemma.

Yet if the concept of leadership in politics is dead, why is there such a persistent preoccupation with those waiting in the wings? The journalistic hobby of successor-spotting is being raised to the status of a high form of art, as radio, television and other media devote disproportionate time and column inches to the men and women who may next occupy centre stage.

Are we then simply in an interregnum? Are we, in fact, yearning for the return of strong leaders who will solve all the insoluble problems, who will right all the wrongs and show us the path towards social and economic Utopias? For as Gershwin put it, 'someone to watch over me'? Maybe, maybe not – but what is certain is the fact that we are still preoccupied with the concept of leadership and of individual leaders, whether we like them or not.

It is the same in the world of work. The rise in the concept of the self-managing team, often coupled with concepts such as delayering and empowerment, has heralded the demise of individual leadership. But is this really the case? If it is, then why do people still queue up to attend leadership programmes? Why do we, as with politics, still find the lives and styles of business leaders fascinating?

So the concept of leadership is not dead, but in many respects it has become a devalued term. It needs to be freed from the clichés and myths with which we have surrounded it and thereby made more accessible to the ordinary man or woman at work. It is something that many can practise in a wide variety of different contexts, and in so doing make a difference to both their own lives and the lives of those around them.

However, if the concept of leadership is not dead, it could be argued that the fashion, or style, of leadership required of those in positions of responsibility has changed and will change further. In doing so, it will make new and perhaps more difficult demands on leaders – especially those who are not at the very pinnacle of their organizations.

We may well be at the uneasy threshold of something new. But if so – what?

Defining leadership in a modern context

In the past, leaders ruled or governed, but more recently the concept of the leader as a servant to his or her followers has gained in popularity. To this day, however, people still try to achieve the definitive meaning of leadership and to separate it from its sister concept of management.

It is certainly not my intention to explore the various definitions here. This has already been done, and I remain happy with the definition I gave in *Discovering the Leader in You*: 'Leadership is something you *do* rather than something you are. It is the ability to bring out a number of talents in yourself and to operate effectively through other people, making them gladly accept your goals while still having the freedom to do things their way. A good leader therefore understands and meets people's positive expectations of how they wish to be led.

Becoming a good leader is something you *choose* to do through a process of action and self-discovery.'

If it is what they do, then *what is it they do* that makes them either effective or ineffective leaders? This question is both tantalizing and exasperating, as we see, in fact, the actions of leaders all the time – either through watching political leaders via the media or by watching our own bosses at work. But actually catching the 'good' in what they do and storing or bottling it for our own use is a different matter. However, if we see something being done well, then we ought to be able to capture and use it. That attitude, skill or competency should be made transferable – it should somehow be made a vehicle for the learning and future effectiveness of others. To misquote Shakespeare: 'the good should *not* be interred with their bones'.

So the definition of the good that leaders do needs to be nailed once and for all. Once thus secured we can put it to pragmatic use.

But first we need to re-examine leadership in the context of today's pressures and dilemmas. The need for leadership or, to put it more precisely, for leaders, to inject meaning or direction into situations is greater than ever. The pace of change accelerates, and with it the multitude of uncertainties, fears, paradoxes and dilemmas that assault us all in both our private and working lives. In some cases it is up to us as individuals to draw our own conclusions and to find our own paths. For example, John Sherer at the PEPI Conference in New Orleans in 1993 said that there were four unavoidable facts of modern life:

1. Your job is not safe.
2. Neither is anything else.
3. Fundamental change and chaos is the new context.
4. What you *used* to do to compensate for change probably won't work this time.

He went on to say that the way to avoid being swamped by the whitewater of modern chaos was to nurture an inner strength and independence that put one on a higher plane. This is fine advice on one spiritual level, but we cannot all exist spiritually and independently the whole time. Most of the time we are forced into interactions and into reliance on others.

Consequently, the need for leadership remains, especially the need for leaders to give meaning to the challenging situations that people face.

So we need leaders and also often need to *be* leaders. Therefore it is necessary to return to the question of 'What is it that effective leaders do?'. In asking that question another question arises, which is whether those actions that leaders undertake can somehow be 'captured' and used to help others. And in reaching that question, the concept of the role model can be seen to be waiting impatiently in the wings.

Leadership is different from management. People react to it in emotional ways and consequently it can be harder to define. I therefore look back in wry amusement when I find myself drawn to one of the driest, most logical and fact-based media to shed further light on this elusive concept, to enable us to revisit the idea of the role model and (above all) to place the whole question into a framework that can be of use to people who want to be better leaders themselves – in other words, to answer the perennial question, 'That's all very well, but *what's in it for me?*'.

The medium in question is that of *competencies*.

Competency or performance?

In Britain the question of whether it was possible to set up a scheme that established national standards of competence against which managers could be evaluated intrigued the Government and some academic administrators. It failed, however, to intrigue many others, including those at whom it was primarily aimed – namely, the army of managers who might have benefited from a professional qualification in 'management' in the way that accountants, lawyers and other 'professionals' have benefited from a vocational qualification in their own specific callings.

In fact, just a mention of the whole concept of National Vocational Qualifications and the Management Charter Initiative is likely to make even the most hardy bureaucrat yawn and look around for a means of escape – a sad end indeed for an initiative that was launched on the back of a unique research effort with the intention of reforming the whole of vocational education. But can the overall concept be more usefully applied to looking at leadership?

There is, of course, a major downside to applying the concept of competencies to leadership. You cannot make a number of ticks on a list and then blithely say, 'Well, I meet enough of the criteria, that proves that I am a leader!'. That is quite frankly nonsense. While it may be possible to check through a list that proves that you are holding down a management job, the concept of leadership is too elusive to be thus quantified. While leadership activities can be listed, it is the *quality and spirit* with which they are undertaken that will indicate whether or not true leadership is present.

If real lessons are to be learned from the application of a competency model to the concept of leadership, the lessons may reside in rewriting and redefining the competencies to better fit the medium we are trying to describe.

So, a rewording of the competencies appeared to be called for. With this in mind, I set out to find a formula that answered both the need to include the factual and tangible as well as the emotional and intangible.

In *Discovering the Leader in You*, I invented a mnemonic to describe the essential qualities or talents of leadership. This was WIST, and the letters stood for:

- *Wisdom*: The ability to exercise judgement, use logic and also to heed one's intuition. It is about being objective while still experiencing emotions.
- *Integrity*: This is about recognizing that even in this age of multiple options and unclear values there are still absolutes connected with honesty, truthfulness and trust. Leaders who disregard them jeopardize their personal credibility.
- *Sensitivity*: This is closely allied to intuition, but is more than that. It is the ability to communicate expertly, to listen well and to be able to put yourself into the other person's shoes when necessary.
- *Tenacity*: Here the talents are concerned with resolution, determination and seeing the task through to the end, despite the odds!

Be WISTful and be powerful. Use the talents incorporated in WIST and be an effective leader – that was the message. The question now arises as to whether the qualities of WIST can be broken down into a wider range of competencies that may be immediately recognized, learned and applied.

A rethinking of WIST, as well as further discussions with colleagues on the subject, came up with the following breakdown, in which the main behavioural elements of WIST are now reproduced.

Leadership Competencies by Grouping

W

Able to create visions of the future – and pursue them.

Intuitive, yet wise in the way that the vision is pursued.

Judges people and situations well.

Has thoughts and opinions on the future of business methods and the nature of work.

Inspiring when necessary. Capable of being a mentor at all times.

Adept at influencing and persuading others.

Aware of the demands of organizational politics – a communicator and networker.

I

Demonstrates to others that they are worthy of trust.

Does not operate on hidden agendas.

Is open and honest in dealings with others.

Does not shrink from candour when necessary.

S (in approach)

Can operate as a coach.

Is a good listener.

Able to empower and develop others.

Understands the power of teams and how to work with them.

Capable of learning continuously.

A facilitator of learning and of situations.

S (in thinking)

Conforming in approach when necessary but capable of non-conformity when appropriate.

Able to handle and embrace diversity of approach and opinion.

Creative – can think outside the box.

Able to think ahead strategically and able to communicate the strategy.

A risk-taker when necessary. Adventurous and courageous.

T

Dynamic, energetic.

Hard-working, yet able to balance work and home life.

Able to cope with pressure.

Capable of handling own stress as well as other people's stress.

Disciplined in own approach to situations. Able to cope with failure and setbacks.

Tenacious – doesn't give up.

Understands and copes with the pressures of power.

Able to handle uncertainty and to help other people do so as well.

Demonstrates optimism when necessary.

Handles change well – plans it and makes it happen.

Having broken down the competencies into elements that made them look much more like talents (something that made me personally feel more comfortable) two questions then arose:

- How should they be tested?

and

- On whom should they be tested?

By implication, it is nearly time to revisit the concept of the role model, as when attempting to answer the second question the outstanding issue in mind was as follows: what benefit to other people would be derived from the tests themselves?

Testing the competencies

The how

The only way to test the competencies, both to see whether they were valid as well as to see whether they actually existed in the attitudes and behaviour of real leaders, was through structured interviews in which the questions sought to test for the WIST competencies. In constructing the questionnaire, I was confronted with a problem. Although I wanted to see whether the interviewees actually possessed them, I did not want the questions asked to signal the answer required. For example, in testing for dynamism and energy it would hardly be appropriate to ask interviewees, 'Are you dynamic and energetic?'. However the answer came, the chances of getting honesty or realism would be minimal.

It was therefore necessary to devise a questionnaire that approached the competencies and talents in a more roundabout way. Even so, it was going to be difficult to test for elements such as integrity, so I set out to construct a questionnaire that would lure the candidates into conversations in which their attitudes, skills and approaches would be exposed and then further elaborated.

Consequently, from the very start the whole approach was unscientific, but, in being so, I hoped that it would more closely capture the very essence of effective leadership.

The questionnaire itself is reproduced in full at the end of the book. It is quite lengthy, and in conducting the interviews I soon found that while it was possible to test for the full range of identified competencies, most individuals appeared to exhibit more of some than of others. This did not necessarily mean that they did not possess all those competencies, but it did indicate that they were stronger in other areas and played to those strengths, either because that is what the situation demanded or because that was the way they were.

The who

The subjects of the interviews were going to be easier to select.

I had already reached the conclusion that the hyper-successful and super-famous were devalued metaphors for leadership, because names such as Branson, Roddick, Trump and Harvey-Jones had been so over-used as to make them devalued currency. More importantly, these people had, by virtue of their success, wealth and fame, distanced themselves so far from more ordinary mortals as to make themselves poor role models. They might well be excellent leaders, but their value as examples is diminished – the leap from examining them to thinking about one's own situation is just too great.

Consequently, I felt strongly that the most telling examples, both of the competencies in action as well as quite simply of good leadership in action, lay with the successful yet unsung leaders at more modest levels: people who had not been changed by fame and fortune – people who were just like you and me.

In selecting my guinea-pigs I set five criteria:

1. They should all be unknown in media terms.
2. They should be successful both in their organizations and as leaders.
3. Ideally, they should not be at the ultimate peak of their organizations. In other words, they should be answerable to someone in the organization as opposed to shareholders or other external agencies.
4. In order to give variety, those chosen should be from a selection of organizations, countries and professions.
5. If someone is considered to be a good leader, he or she should be supremely good at one or more aspects of leading. The people chosen ought to be powerful examples of at least one of the talents under examination and thus have distinct lessons for other people through their views, attitudes or actions.

This does not mean that my guinea-pigs are in any way banal or boring. In fact, I hope that they are the very opposite. They include a Senior Civil Servant facing up to the fact that his department, which was once totally secure, was pitched into the commercial stream due to the phenomenon of market testing; an ex-military man whose job is now to lead teams involved in negotiations to free kidnap victims; and a senior insurance manager who started life in England as an Indian 'imported bride' who scarcely knew her husband or the ways of her new country.

The one factor that I consider them all to have in common is that their stories have messages for the reader. The examples of what they have done *and are still doing* carry lessons that can be put into place in the reader's own job function. They are relevant!

Before starting to interview my guinea-pigs, I asked myself what conclusions my small yet diverse sample of leaders was likely to produce. Would they shed new light on the subject? Would they, on the other hand, show that the very nature of modern leadership was changing? Or would they indicate that people tended to lead in much the same way as before and that there was, in fact, nothing new under the sun?

On the other hand, would my candidates illustrate sufficient levels of self-knowledge to know exactly what they were doing, how they were doing it and what the likely outcomes of their actions would be? There were no easy answers to these questions. That my candidates would illustrate many of the competencies, I had little doubt. Of the fact that their lives, views and experiences would well illustrate the mysterious concept of leadership and be worthwhile examples to other people, I had even less doubt.

My initial hypotheses, however, were that:

1. The more competencies in which a leader readily showed a strength, the more likely that person would be considered a good leader.
2. That a shift in the nature of leadership is taking place, with modern leaders increasingly having to take on new roles, skills and attitudes in order to be effective in changing business environments.

However, to return to the concept of bottling – how would the competencies be tested and illustrated, with lessons then being extracted for the reader in a way that would be both relevant and meaningful? Or, to put it bluntly, how would value for money be obtained from the unsung heroes and heroines?

The structure

The main guarantee for assuring value for money seemed to lie in imposing a common structure on all the interview reports. Doing that would enable the reader to make constant comparisons between both the different interview subjects and their own particular leadership situations. Consequently, the structure of the interview-based chapters is as follows:

1. Description of the leader, name, role and function in the organization.
2. The subject's organization as the overall context of his or her endeavours and activities. Description of what is happening there and the challenges that they represent to that person.
3. What the subject has achieved to date and what he or she hopes to achieve in the future.
4. Description of the main points of interest arising from the interview. (While each person was interviewed according to the same format, it was not my intention to reproduce each interview in full but rather to concentrate on those particular talents and competencies that that person uniquely brings to the party and on which they concentrate during the interviews. This I hope will ensure greater variety and readability while allowing the reader to focus on the particular lessons that each subject may have to pass on.)
5. Finally, in each case the messages for the reader will be summarized and any particular lessons emerging about the nature of modern leadership further elaborated.

To help the individual who wishes to learn from the unsung heroes and heroines, I suggest that, in conjunction with thinking about particular challenges, you adopt the following structure for a form of self-audit in terms of your own future development.

1. *Awareness*: Am I aware that there may be new attitudes or behaviours demanded of me from an examination of these people and that I may need to change?

2. *Integration*: How can I integrate these new demands into my approach to leading? What is required of me to do so?
3. *Examination*: As I embark on the road to new activities or approaches, how is it going? Are they working for me, or do I need to do more, or less, in some areas?
4. *Emphasis*: If the new behaviours or attitudes are working for me and *are* making a difference, can I then emphasize them by doing them or demonstrating them more frequently and even better as my experience grows?

Summary

The challenge in adopting an approach that is even loosely tied to the concept of competencies is to make the competencies themselves come alive and have meaning for others. The MCI movement has been the object of much criticism and may or may not succeed as an approach to looking at managerial work. In examining the more elusive concept of leadership, it is hoped that a redefinition of competencies along new lines may not only shed further light on leadership but also revitalize and perhaps even humanize the concept of competencies.

However, more important than the competencies are the guinea-pigs, the interview subjects. They are all living, working people, subject to the same pressures as the great and the good, but probably far more vulnerable and hence possibly more human. Bill Drath of the Center for Creative Leadership described the context of work as like an ocean with white-headed waves emerging from it. The waves were the leaders – they stood out, but never ceased to be part of the overall context. The particular leaders identified here stand out as individuals for a time but never cease to be part of the overall context of ongoing leadership in this changing and uncertain world.

CHAPTER 2

Nicholas Boothman
The push for competitive commerciality

Introduction

If pushed, Nick Boothman will admit to being a civil servant, but that is where it ends.

Although he is, in fact, a very senior civil servant, we are not looking at the traditional Whitehall mandarin in a pinstripe suit – the sort that discusses fiscal policy in a gentlemanly fashion in the hallowed halls of the Treasury. Nothing could be further from the truth!

This may imply that Nick Boothman is not a gentleman (he most certainly is), but there are many different versions of that sublime concept, and Boothman does not fit the standard 'Sir Humphrey' model one iota. As Director of Technology of the Metropolitan Police's Department of Technology (DoT), he is at the head of a substantial business, and one that has been subjected to greater demands for change in the last five years than most businesses have faced in the last two decades.

But what of the man?

Boothman is a short, stocky individual in his early fifties. Balding, cheerful and a favourer of brown suits and knitted ties rather than traditional city garb, he has a ready smile that can belie the determination underneath. He likes to be approachable, enjoying discussion, and worries when more junior people are diffident about approaching him.

The DoT is housed in a faceless office in Pimlico, London, with other satellite offices in south London that are shared with Government departments of varying degrees of secrecy and anonymity. Boothman's corner office looks out towards the Thames in one direction and west towards Battersea in the other. It is from here that he directs the Department, treading a demanding tightrope between business management, political influence and being principal change agent in a culture that has traditionally only embraced technological change reluctantly and which now demands a sensitive touch to steer it through what could still be very troubled waters.

The context

The DoT exists to provide professional technological support and associated services to meet the needs of the Metropolitan Police Service (MPS). This support ranges from providing police vehicles of various shapes and sizes through to providing 'listening devices' and walkie-talkies. The Department coordinates major projects with external technology companies to introduce projects such as computerized vehicle tracking systems, and is responsible for the technology that is used by the command and control systems.

The DoT maintains live computer systems that operate 24 hours a day, 365 days a year. These include Computer-Aided Despatch (the 999 service); the Message Switch System, which covers administration messages and special messages for the police; the police action computer; and a system known as METOPS, used for tracking special operations such as the Notting Hill Carnival or Trooping the Colour. The mainframe computers and software are maintained by teams of people made up of DoT staff and contract staff from organizations such as Unisys and EDS.

The pace of technological change is fast and demanding, for the DoT is currently examining the future demands of command and control. Touch-screens are being installed to speed up response times and direct data communication with police vehicles is also being evaluated, while in hand is the upgrading of the central computers and core software.

In short, the DoT is a highly complex organization employing approximately 2000 people and engaged in a wide variety of multi-million pound projects. It is also an organization that is under threat from changing government philosophies that affect the very heart of the way that public authorities, local government and civil service departments run.

Boothman's aim and prime challenge has been to ensure that the DoT remains a crucial and wanted part of the MPS's infrastructure, providing a service well into the 21st century.

The challenge

The MPS has been going through a period of considerable change, with a number of reports and measures either in place or up for debate designed to give better effectiveness and value for money in the delivery of policing services to the public. These have included the controversial Sheehy report, the recommendations of the Royal Commission on Criminal Justice and the Police Bill, all of which have had an impact on the MPS's thinking.

Although the MPS is not able to operate as a profit-making business (thank goodness!), the culture within it is becoming closer to that more usually found in the commercial sector, where the internal customer has greater freedom of choice over the supply and purchase of goods and services. An increased emphasis on performance is being placed on those parts of the organization that provide these services, and this impacts directly on the DoT.

As an integral part of the MPS, yet separate from it, the DoT has a unique understanding of how the use of technology increases the effectiveness of police officers. However, it is already being asked to provide a stronger focus on the delivery of a total quality service to its prime customer, as well as to prove that it is totally cost-effective in providing this support.

Of course, under the government-sponsored initiative known as 'market testing', whereby central and local agencies have to prove that they can deliver services efficiently and cost-effectively, the threat connected with under-performance is very real, as the internal customer can now walk away and buy from an external source. With the amount of publicity given to the market testing initiative and the richness of the pickings from what competitors would see as fat cats, Boothman and some of his colleagues saw the vultures circling.

In 1992, Boothman and his Board decided that there was no point in waiting for events to unfold, or for the Government to unveil more plans in an atmosphere of uncertainty; it was preferable to step out to meet the anticipated new demands. Initially, this would mean identifying current business costs, making plans to develop a new relationship with the prime customers in the MPS and devolving decisions about spending and project management further down the line.

Boothman summarized the future demands in the DoT's business plan. 'Our future success depends crucially on meeting the needs of our clients both inside and outside the MPS at a price which represents best value for money to the customer. How we present ourselves and the products and skills we have to offer will be key factors in shaping our future and survival.'

To achieve this success it was obvious to Boothman that a shared vision had to be developed about the future direction of the Department, so that all staff would feel able to contribute to its development and earn a share in its success. At the same time, Boothman recognized that this required the Board to have a clearer focus on the skills that would be required within the DoT and to develop plans to match individuals to those skills.

Another crucial problem was that while Boothman and some of his Board had a reasonably clear overview of the situation and the implied threats, this was by no means the case with the majority of his managerial and technical staff. Thus, faced with the size of the challenge confronting the DoT and the need for swift positive action, Boothman sought external help. A process was begun.

A process for change

In order to understand the process better, it is first necessary to look more closely at the type of people that were to be involved in it.

While the DoT is an adjunct to the MPS, its staff are all civil servants, holding definable civil service ranks and gradings rather than police rankings. A comfortable civil service mentality prevailed. There was a tradition of long service within the DoT, and most staff members could look back a long time over years where the customer had had no choice but to come to them. This does not mean that they were sloppy or disrespectful of the customer, but it does mean that there was no history of competitive customer service against other potential suppliers – the type of situation that sharpens business acumen and breeds a different form of culture within the organization.

At the same time, most staff were technical experts who were primarily focused on products rather than sales or service. At the top, within Boothman's Board, there were some strong characters, and views were set for polarization between the ethos of 'we must move now and move fast – whatever it is that we end up doing' and the philosophy of 'Yes, change is probably necessary, but fast movement may well botch the job so we had better wait and see how things develop'. Coupled together these opinions were a sure-fire recipe for frustrated inaction!

In the past, the DoT had held an annual conference at which future issues were discussed. A certain level of staff involvement had prevailed at these events, but for the 1993 conference Boothman wanted to tackle fully what he considered to be the most pressing agenda for future years and to involve his teams in both setting and actioning that agenda. It was with this in mind that he approached the P.A. Sundridge Park consultancy and thus started a profitable partnership that is still ongoing at the time of writing.

Consultants from Sundridge Park designed a programme that aimed to shake up the DoT participants and make them face up to the demands of the future, examine their own mind sets and also discuss how, as teams, they could best implement the future actions they were helping to plan.

Elements of the programme included:

- *Analysis*: Where are we now?
- *Discussion*: What is needed for the future?
  What is meant by customer focus?
  What does it mean for us?
- *Techniques*: Looking at creative options
  Projects as a means of implementing change
- *Planning and implementation*
- *Selection of projects for change*

To say that the three days of the event were stormy would be a gross understatement. Many participants felt that the view of the future being painted was unpalatable or that, by implication, the suggestion that they had to focus more strongly on their customers was insulting. Nevertheless, out of this process were born a number of 'Projects for Change' which examined the very core of the way that the DoT organized itself to do business.

Board level initiatives

Thereafter, it was up to the Board to examine how it could best support the Projects for Change by better playing to its own strengths, working together as a team and producing an agreed vision for the future that would underpin future strategy and help it meet the client's expectations. But first it had to understand those expectations more fully.

To help it reach those goals, Sundridge Park designed a series of Board team-building and strategy workshops at which these key priorities were, one by one, addressed. These workshops were characterized by a lot of plain speaking and much hard work. At times they were painful (when examination of team roles showed where gaps needed to be addressed), and at times they were exhilarating, when real progress was made or when the vision for the future shape of the DoT became clearer. Possibly the most exciting occasions were when senior police officers took part in the workshops, so that both sides could share their perceptions and expectations of one another. These visits were motivating when it became clear, on the first occasion, that expectations were being met, and sobering when, on the second visit, the police officers stated that they would have liked to have seen more progress in the interim.

Throughout this process, Boothman made sure that the decisions of the workshops were put into practice within the DoT. In many respects, the workshops were merely the tip of the iceberg, as reorganization continued apace. New structures were announced, a small redundancy programme took place and a new senior appointment was made, and amid continuing debate at both Board and more junior levels the DoT moved towards its future.

Behind this whole process was the energetic figure of Nick Boothman – the enthusiastic yet compassionate change agent: a man who sometimes struggles to keep his distance from problems, even when he knows that they should be delegated, a man who will face up to conflict but lie awake all night before firing somebody, a man who has the confidence of a person who knows that he is good, but who still has the humility to seek external help on running his Board meetings and who accepts that he sometimes needs a mentor. What of the man himself?

What does Boothman think, feel and do? What talents and competencies does he display and what do those around him think of him?

Background

By training, Nick Boothman is a physicist, and attributes much of his success in later life to the disciplines he learned as a student.

He concludes that physics, never an easy subject, forces the student to be analytical and to be a *synthesizer*. By this, he means that the scientific processes employed within the subject force the person trying to find answers to break down problems and to analyse them in manageable bits. This means that few problems appear too large or, in the end, too complex to be dealt with. It enables the individual to remain calm and objective, and above all to achieve the valuable helicopter overview that results in good decision-making based on knowing the choice of options open.

A talent within Boothman is the ability to analyse why and how his past experiences have helped him and how to use them in the future. 'You have to be self-reliant in physics', he concludes, 'only you can solve the problems in the end'. He ruminates that it is a pity that more students do not actively analyse how their course of study, and the way that they approach it, can assist them in their later careers.

Boothman's first job was in GEC Research, where his physics training was put to work. However, the lack of a commercial approach within research frustrated him, and he migrated towards the product end of the business – to project-based development, which was very commercial.

Later in his career he moved to the user side of commercial project management when he joined the Ministry of Defence (MoD). As the recipient of a wide range of technical defence-based projects, the MoD was extremely advanced in ensuring the quality of the work that it received, and Boothman turned his side of its operations into a formidable outfit by insisting that it added project management skills to its existing ability to control projects from the purchaser's end.

When he joined the DoT as Senior Engineer in 1977, Boothman was able to bring all his experience of both being a provider and a user of technical projects to the job. He became the Project Manager for the huge Command and Control project in 1980. This project, which broadly centred around the concept of the installation of a computer system being used to handle 999 calls and other police force messaging, was one of the largest and most complex conceived to date. It was to cost approximately £25 million over its first 10 years, and taught Boothman the value of courage when, as with all projects, there were crises and alarms during its development.

There are times, he concludes when you just have to accept that there are risks, accept that they are part of the job and that it is part of your job to live with them and help others to do so as well. This was, in fact, about being courageous and displaying that courage for others to see. Sometimes the staff's spirits were kept up by social events, such as river trips, but often Boothman had to accept the responsibility of leadership and continue in the faith that a solution would always be found in the end. There were times, however, when he was forced to accept that a loss of sleep for two nights in a week was just par for the course.

Boothman is philosophical about the tough times. Work, life and leadership are all about learning, and while you value the lessons of your student days, in the end there is 'no classroom like just having to do it!'.

After completing his stint on the Command and Control project, Boothman did a two-year spell in a staff job which gave him time to think, survey the overall context in which the DoT was operating and look ahead. When he was promoted to Chief Engineer, he was convinced that a big change was on its way, and he also had a good understanding of the probable demands that this change would impose and what the likely timings would be. He concluded that he had three and a half years to get himself ready, prepare the DoT and build the team with which he would lead the way through these changes.

With almost poetic timing, he was appointed Director of Technology, which placed him in the position of chief executive of the DoT, just as the first real changes arrived – the series of events described earlier in this chapter then ensued.

Challenge, influence and achievements

Boothman sees the main challenge currently facing him as having to establish the positioning of the DoT within the vast, complex organization that is the Metropolitan Police Service. Although qualifying in terms of size alone as a medium to large organization, it is but a small part of the overall MPS, and not regarded by very many officers as core to the business. In addition, it is necessary to sort out the Department's interfaces with the MPS, to check how its management style fits in with that of the MPS and, through ongoing checks and communication, to ensure that it is equipped to fulfil its function.

In order to meet this challenge, Boothman has consciously to be an influencer, and he sees his battles as an influencer being fought on three fronts.

1. *Current staff*: the necessity to influence and carry on influencing the people in the DoT. There is still some fear of change and suspicion that what is proposed to bring the

Department into the future is not really necessary. To overcome this view, Boothman has consistently hammered home the message that 'the only continuing certainty is continuing change'. Once people realize this, he concludes, they are much happier about accepting it and will help to achieve progress.

2. *Top management*: this is represented by the Policy Committee of the MPS, which is chaired by Britain's top policeman, Sir Paul Condon. He sees his role here as helping the committee's members to see both the current and potential place for the DoT within the MPS. Boothman also considers that the Policy Committee should have an advisory role in helping him understand the right place for the Department within the MPS, and understands that it is up to him to persuade them to give him this advice.
3. *Stakeholders in the DoT*: these are represented by the Home Office and the rest of the criminal justice business. Here the job is to educate them and make them realize that they *are* stakeholders and what this should mean for them in terms of ongoing support.

Looking back over the last two years, Boothman states that the DoT has nearly been changed from being technology-led to being business-led. Furthermore, he has also built teams that are now starting to work.

Success breeds success, and the market has been stimulated, if not overstimulated. The question that now arises is whether the Department can meet the total demand. Boothman now sees a further challenge in trying to capture the market in depth. Police chiefs may see the merits of what the DoT is trying to do, but ordinary police officers still moan about their equipment and the battle will not be won until these people understand what the DoT is trying to do for them.

At the top power level there are still battles to be fought, but Boothman feels that success is within his grasp, and the question that now stands is: has the vision been achieved?

Manager and leader

What follows is drawn from the discussions with Nick Boothman based around the competencies tested by the Portable Leader Questionnaire.

So, did he have a vision for the DoT?

Here Boothman's reply is an interesting contrast to the approach identified by many leaders. He did have a vision for the future of the organization, but it was a vision of principle rather than exact detail.

The principle was that the DoT needed to change its approach – the very nature of the way that it did business and managed projects. This was not just about being effective, it was about survival, and a personal part of his vision was that others within the DoT should feel the same.

The actual process of making the vision happen was pursued via the sequence of both internal and facilitated events described earlier in this chapter, and Boothman needed to walk the tightrope of planning which decisions could be made by the whole management team, which should be made and owned by the board and which fell to him alone. It was also a question of pacing himself, as he realized from the start that the process and his passion for the eventual outcome would consume him to a large degree.

In order to help spread the load and also because he passionately believed that this was the right approach, Boothman encouraged dialogue and debate. In fact, he soon found that his people thrived on the debate. It was when it subsided that things began to go wrong, and the question arises as to whether the dialogue and sharing of ideas that it provoked meant that everybody became better informed and consequently were able to make better decisions, even if at that time they were not yet fully convinced.

That probably did apply, but there were other, more powerful, forces at work. Somehow the debate became the liberator of minds. One board member, who had previously managed projects in Saudi Arabia, openly stated that if it were not for Boothman and his approach he would be back in the Middle East. Boothman reflects that a major part of his role as a change agent has been to inject both high excitement and high activity into communication, exploration and process. It is the combination of those two elements that both starts and keeps people going.

There were downsides, and these emphasized the need for the process to be a shared one. A major personal lesson that Nick Boothman learned during this time was that energy is not infinite. It is a precious commodity, and the effective leader must learn to conserve it and be able to regenerate it. During the gaps it helps enormously if others are sufficiently empowered to commit their energy, thereby keeping up the momentum. In this case, the supply of 'others' was plentiful.

Did Boothman feel that he had been inspirational, and what was his understanding of the term? To Boothman, inspiration is about ideas, enjoyment and recognition.

The ideas are vital, but it is not only up to the leader to have the ideas (that would be counterproductive); in an environment where creativity has historically not been the main requirement, it is the job of the leader to infect others with the *courage* to have the right ideas and to try to make them reality. Boothman strongly believes that it was the fact that he clearly showed his enjoyment of the change process and excitement in it that infected others with the will to contribute ideas. Indeed, Boothman is quick to stress the value of communicated excitement. It is this excitement about the opportunities that drives him on as well as many of his staff. He considers that feelings of stress and excitement are very similar, and wonders whether those who cannot deal with stress are also adverse to excitement.

But it took more than enjoyment to make it happen. It was necessary to give the credit to people when they had ideas, to mark their achievements publicly and to demonstrate his enthusiasm for what they had done. It took a very physical gesture to show his team that he was prepared to let go and not have a hand in everything that was going on.

Boothman's office occupies a prime corner site at Drummond Gate, and he had placed his desk facing the door so that from it he could see down the corridor – and be seen. By moving his desk to a corner of his office, so that he could neither see or be seen, he sent a powerful message to his people: the boss was standing back, and wanted his people to get on with it without constant reference to him.

At the same time, he let it be known that he would always defend them when they stepped out with a worthwhile initiative. The customers in the MPS had a historic reputation for not taking prisoners when it came to disagreements, and Boothman more than once had to stand his ground and say 'I'm not allowing you to say that about him!'. This was a risky policy at a time when it was necessary to work on the provider/client relationship, but Boothman felt it was a worthwhile risk. Integrity was vital, and it had to be demonstrated in all directions.

There were times when Boothman had to encourage risk-taking among his project leaders, and found that it paid dividends to say, 'Yes, there *is* a risk, but I'm sharing it with you and will go down before you if things go wrong'. This approach was especially necessary when the CRIS (Criminal Records Information System) Project was 'wobbly' – and it worked, as the project was to succeed, mainly due to the perseverance and courage of a few middle ranking project managers.

And when success comes, Boothman is adamant that it is not up to him to take any credit. 'Give the credit away', he says emphatically, 'give it to individuals and sometimes give it to the client, or other organizations if you feel that it has been earned'.

Facing up to the problems

It is all too easy to be glib when it comes to talking about 'the vision'. At quite a late stage in the change process, differences of approach arose in the Board.

These differences centred on different views about and interpretations of what sort of culture should be encouraged in the DoT and around what sort of organization should underpin that culture. To compound the situation, a new high-level appointment from outside the organization had emphasized the need for more of a marketing approach and the reorganization implicit within that concept.

While earlier workshops had concentrated on getting commitment to the vision by letting those involved in its implementation develop it, the Board now felt it necessary to go back to basics, and they asked a number of fundamental questions.

1. What was the difference between mission and vision?
2. What in fact was organizational culture, and how could it be identified?
3. Where did values enter the equation?
4. How would the Board need to act to demonstrate the consistent values that would underpin the future of the DoT?
5. What changes in both organization and Board behaviour were necessary?

These questions provoked brisk debate at a post-Christmas Board retreat. Feathers were ruffled when differences were aired about what sort of culture people actually wanted, but in the end there was a degree of consensus, and in time the team became stronger for having been through the conflict.

Boothman, in looking at problems, is very matter of fact. 'Be prepared to throw things out and start again if they are not working', he states, 'but have everybody involved in that decision and in the replanning.' Fortunately, that was not necessary in this case.

When it comes to problem-solving, Boothman recognizes the value of an intuitive approach, but as a scientist he does not always allow himself the luxury of using his intuition. In fact, it often takes his PA to nudge him into an intuitive frame of mind by asking, 'What do you feel in your water about it?'. Where Boothman does score, however, is in his willingness to accept help from others when there are problems. 'You can get help from all sorts of places', he says, 'and I have learned not to be too proud either to ask for it or to accept it.' This humility probably compensates for his occasional unwillingness to be intuitive.

The politician

The context of the DoT, with its relationship to the MPS and other Civil Service departments, is one where organizational politics can thrive. However, it is here that Nick Boothman admits to being most diffident. He is quite a shy person, and this makes it harder for him to make the contacts and connections that he believes are necessary to prosper politically. Paradoxically, perhaps, this shyness works in his favour, as he firmly believe that if you approach people reasonably they will react reasonably to you and be prepared to form alliances. Furthermore, when he lists the people he knows, both in government and in commerce, the benefits of having a 'reasonable approach' soon become apparent.

An instance when all of Boothman's abilities as a politician and an influencer were apparent was when he found it necessary to fight for the Metropolitan Police Radio Project against Home Office opposition. He felt that the civil servants in the Home Office had a reasonable agenda, but it 'was not the DoT's'. In order to bring key decision-makers around to his way of thinking, he needed to keep speaking to the right people – to convince them. It was a matter of keeping the channels open and investing heavily in his own time and energy to win them around.

When it comes to internal politics, Boothman has a different strategy. He firmly believes that it is his job to draw the sting out of them. Although he knows when and how to be tough, and has sometimes had to be so (for example when the CRIS project was once in difficulty and his boss would not allow him to invest in the installation of proper project management to bring it around), he much prefers to stop people clashing by saying 'It's really not that important'. Over and above this he transmits a personal credo of 'I want to do it right and I need to know what is the right approach'. Over the years, he has fostered a reputation of getting close to 'the right approach' and of then doing it right. It is hard to be political in the face of this applied perfectionism, and it is helpful that Jim Clifton, his number two, has the same credo, which means that, even when there is conflict between them, they both know that in the end they have the same values and are somehow seeking the same conclusion.

On the subject of power, Boothman is equally candid. He does not think of his job in terms of power, even though he obviously has it. He rejects the notion of 'when I say jump, jump!'. Even the main line police force still has this image. A more compelling paradigm, he says, is that of thinking of your job in terms of its sphere of influence and of your personal capability to make a difference within that sphere.

Integrity and trust

As a leader, Nick Boothman believes in three vital concepts – values, trust and the consistency of their application.

The leader, he states, needs to be candid, as this will show others what your values actually are, but being candid should not mean that you are constantly meeting others in head-on collisions. Although, in extreme cases, you may have to be direct in the expression of your views, being over-blunt probably will not help, as in the long run relationships must continue.

He considers that there is a fine line to be drawn. People have to trust you, and you need to say enough to build that trust. On the other hand, you cannot always say everything, and you need to tell people when you are not prepared to go any further, as being perceived as manipulative is bound to lose you ground. The ability to manoeuvre your way through this particular dilemma is the cornerstone of applied integrity. Boothman adds that there is a direct causal link between a wish to 'do it right' and the urge for leadership. Those who succeed strike a balance between putting this design into action and maintaining their integrity.

And then there is the concept of consistency, which when applied to the expression of values is the cornerstone of applied integrity. An example that Boothman gives here comes from an occasion when he was experiencing difficulty with one senior person. Some time before, he had given this individual assurances that he would support him through difficult times. Quite shortly after this, Boothman came under extreme pressure from senior levels to remove this person. Even though the way was made clear for a swift and easy removal, Boothman resisted both the pressures and the temptation, choosing to stick by his word. In the longer term, this strategy paid off, not only in terms of the individual concerned, who was grateful, but also in the eyes of those who had exerted the pressure.

Empowerment, rules and facilitation

As in the case of integrity, which does not mean much until it is applied, Boothman considers empowerment to be little more than a buzz-word until somebody does something about it and wonders how many leaders positively *do* practise empowerment.

The whole process of the engineered culture shift of the DoT to a more client-focused footing he considers to have been one of increasing empowerment: taking people from a position where they were afraid of the implied changes and consequently unwilling to take a lead in applying them to one where they were keen to be driving the process forward. This change of spirit took place in under two years, and the formation of supportive project teams that worked was seen to be integral and underpinned everything. The move towards empowerment was characterized by the items on the programme of an internal Heads of Branches meeting held in December 1994.

Agenda items for this day-long event, which involved the same 40 managers who had attended the difficult opening meeting in February 1993, were as follows:

Head of Branches Meeting

1. Scene Setting. N Boothman 0900–0930
2. Involvement of Branch Heads in the Management Process. (Empowerment)

   External facilitator will explain what he understands empowerment to mean. This will be followed by syndicates defining what empowerment means to them and how they would wish to be empowered. Session ends with syndicate report backs.

3. Team Work

   External facilitator will open by explaining characteristics of effective teams. Syndicates will then identify what team work means to them, whether they see the DoT as an effective team and what can be done to increase teamwork in it.

4. Responding to Customer Needs

   Division into two groups. Each group to look at the above issue from a different perspective.

   A From the DoT point of view.

   B From the customer's point of view.

   Each group to report back and make recommendations.

5 Open Session

   The following questions to be debated.

   a Where have we come from?

   b Where are we now?

   c Where are we going to and is it where we want to be?

   d How do we get to where we want to be?

Nick Boothman concluded the day with a review in which he emphasized his wish to involve managers in key issues of strategy and planning. In fact, the final questions addressed in the open session were very much aimed at empowering the managers by introducing them to the questions to be asked when entering the strategic planning process.

At the event Boothman had involved an external facilitator, and although the role here had been subcontracted out so that it would not look as if he was trying to steer the groups towards his conclusions, he is a believer in facilitation as something that the modern leader must do. He considers facilitation to mean the setting up of an environment in which people can contemplate difficult problems with confidence and handle the dissent that may arise without recourse to higher authority. At times it may only be up to the leader to ask the question, 'What should we do in this situation? After that it is up to the others to come up with the ideas, and up to the leader to listen to them'.

Boothman, for a civil servant, is remarkably ambivalent about rules and regulations when looking at them with his facilitator's hat on. He concedes that most rules are in place to help you rather than to hinder, and if looked at creatively the barriers that they appear to impose usually disappear. He considers that it is his job to create the atmosphere in which people look at rules in a positive way. By encouraging creative approaches to rules, which in turn gives birth to the excitement that results in energetic action, he feels that much can be achieved within the overall spirit of the law.

Strategy and stress

Boothman's overall strategy has been to change radically the way in which the DoT has approached the market and its principal customer. The immediate aim has been for the DoT to become the obvious 'one-stop shop' for the MPS. In the longer term new opportunities may well arise, and he knows that the organization must both anticipate what they might be and be ready for them when they arise. Ideally, the new opportunities should be little more than milestones on a path that the DoT is already treading.

In formulating strategy, Boothman is aware that it is necessary to think in terms of values and culture. He realizes that he has been the cause of the new culture within the DoT, and he now appreciates the level of commitment that was demanded of him when he was influencing it. 'You must totally believe in the new culture', he states emphatically. 'If you have even the smallest misgivings about whether it is right and you allow these misgivings to be known, then it won't survive'. For him the values and culture become the same thing.

In some respects it is not difficult for Boothman to think strategically about the organization as he 'eats, drinks and talks the DoT' for most of his waking life. There are, of course, dangers here. The working day is reserved for doing the immediate work, and much of the remaining time is spent in thinking and planning. Wryly, he concedes that if he did not get extreme satisfaction from the job he would be in a fix. However, the satisfaction is there, and Boothman believes that to be strategic you must be well ahead with your thinking. He considers it necessary to dismantle situations in your mind and rebuild them to see if they still look right. He draws diagrams of situations and always looks to see what can be learned from them, and then looks to see whether the answer can be built into solving a larger problem.

Boothman concedes that he cannot just switch on the strategic thinking. He can solve workaday problems but not address strategic issues. For this to happen he needs to relax, and he realizes that his committed approach imposes on him the need to manage his energy carefully – otherwise he is in danger of drying up creatively. Like so many people, he finds that his best ideas come when he is not imposing creativity on himself. For example, he plays the violin in a chamber quartet and can let his mind wander – often to see the way ahead more clearly.

This does not mean that Boothman is immune from stress. He admits that most stress is self-imposed, and often involves seeing problems that simply do not exist. Sometimes he finds himself anticipating viewpoints from people that they simply do not hold 'you can overestimate your importance in other people's universes', he muses. 'Often the problem or anticipated objection just does not arise.'

Although he does get stressed by those things beyond his control (what he refers to as the impersonal political drivers), he believes that they should not stress him too much and should not hijack a strategy, even though they must be taken into consideration. It is worthwhile remembering the old adage '*que sera, sera*', he reflects, 'and sometimes I find it necessary to give myself a good talking to!'.

Summary and conclusions

To coin the modern term, Boothman has made the paradigm shift. What is more important, he has altered other people's views of their organization and the commercial possibilities open to it. In doing so, Boothman has demonstrated courage and tenacity in pushing for what he believed had to happen, but at the same time has shown compassion for those who were finding the process difficult.

On another level, Boothman has perhaps unconsciously managed the process of *healing* in an organization that has gone through major changes. Although never too proud to seek external help in changing attitudes, the internal projects for change actively empowered staff at all levels.

Where Boothman differs from many leaders is the degree to which he has had to act as a representative of his organization. This has forced him to seek a balance of views and objectivity, and it has also shown that it is perfectly possible to be politically 'cute', even if shy.

Finally, Boothman has a lesson for us all. Good leaders should think about their leadership role and on the lessons from their past experience and education that they can bring to bear to help with the demands of the present. Here, by fully allowing the reflective side of his nature to reign supreme, he is a 'past master' and consequently master of the present!

Key strengths and portable qualities

- Ability to recognize the changing scenario and its demands on the business.
- Identify need for a new culture which must be underpinned by changed mind sets – and then acted out.
- Retains compassion, even under pressure.
- Remembers lessons from the past, but continues to learn from the present.
- Sees need for leader to be an influence at all levels.
- Recognizes that motivation can come about through debate and communication of the leader's *excitement* about the future.
- Knows how to retain integrity under a variety of pressures.
- Recognizes the prime need for the leader to be customer-focused.
- Is a change agent but also manages the process of 'post-change healing'.

CHAPTER 3

Karuna Sood
Much more than just another sales manager

Introduction

In this chapter, in contrast with the others, the main lesson lies in the story told by the central character rather than in what that person has said about leadership or illustrated via his or her actions. Consequently, many of the messages of this chapter will be different, although none the less valuable for that.

As a story, there is a happy ending, although perhaps it would be more accurate to say 'a happy interim', as the central character is still very much alive and kicking, and at best only half-way through her overall story. As tales go, this is one about achievement, but more than that, it is about having the will and perseverance to succeed in career terms and, in doing so, to become a leader. This is a true story that focuses on the T in WIST, and if, having read it, the reader considers an element of luck to have been present, even the least charitable would concede that in the end we make our own luck and that tenacity, perseverance and downright doggedness have played a major part in making it in this case.

The person

I first met Karuna Sood when she was sent on one of our Leadership in Management Programmes at Sundridge Park in early 1991. This is a programme that aims to develop leadership skills in 'new' leaders or in those for whom the people management side of their job has significantly expanded. It is an intensive, challenging experience for participants, and as programme manager it was my job to keep an eye on both their learning and their well-being.

Amidst the dozen or so participants, mainly white and male on this particular iteration of the programme, was a young Indian woman in her early thirties who had been sent to us by Churchill Insurance, a rapidly growing telephone sales-based motor insurance company. As Churchill had grown, the trickle of people attending our programmes had increased to a steady stream, and Karuna Sood was one of several people that I had met from that organization.

She managed to exude a familiarity with Western culture without in any way sacrificing the manners of her Asian background. At first she appeared somewhat diffident, perhaps wondering what was lying in wait during the week to come. On being asked how many people reported to her she paused to reflect before saying, 'About sixty'. As the week progressed, however, she swiftly changed and was soon contributing as much as, if not more than, any other participant.

I met Karuna Sood again nearly two years later when she returned to Sundridge Park for our more senior leadership programme, Strategic Leadership for Results. In the interim she had clearly matured in terms of her overall confidence and business experience. Again I asked her how many people she led. 'Oh, about three hundred', came the reply. I immediately guessed that there was a story here, as by then I was planning this book, and in speaking to her in greater depth I discovered that there indeed was a story – and a powerful one at that. Initially, Sood declared herself 'too shy to be interviewed and unworthy anyway'. Fortunately, she later changed her mind.

In order to appreciate the Sood story it is, however, first necessary to understand the business environment in which she operates.

Churchill Insurance

Churchill Insurance, which is a leader and originator in the field of telesales insurance, is a lively, unconventional marketing-oriented business in an industry not normally noted for such qualities. Specializing in motor insurance, it claims that careers in the organization are definitely not for pedestrians. Since starting in 1989 with 80 people, it now has over 1000 staff and a turnover in excess of £200 million.

The organization stresses that its success to date stems from an unshakeable belief in the commercial value of excellent customer service, and it is a belief that staff who wish to succeed with Churchill need to embrace.

Karuna Sood is a cog in the machine of change. It is people like her who are instrumental in breaking down the old ways and implementing the new, even if she is not one of the strategic thinkers who are making it happen at the conceptual level.

Karuna Sood's story

Karuna was born the youngest child of a well-to-do family in Kanpur, India.

Her earliest memories are of the atmosphere at home, which, although happy, was extremely traditional and paternalistic. Her father believed in the old order, and that there was a defined place for everything – including daughters. Coeducational schooling was frowned upon as giving all the wrong messages, and the law was clearly laid down at home as to what was permissible and what was not. The family, however, was a close unit and affectionate.

Despite the fact that her early years were restricted and narrow in focus, Karuna showed considerable promise academically, and soon got ahead of her peers. At the age of 14 she sat and passed her O Levels, the usual age in India for this level of achievement being 16, and then went on to do her A Levels. During her studies for O Level she decided that she wanted to become a doctor. On reflection, she feels that this was due more to a strong desire to work with people than due to any deep-seated love of medicine. However, given the restricted nature of her upbringing, the number of role models for her to consider when comparing the variety of options that might be open to her was extremely limited.

The desire to work with people was in direct contrast to the fact that Sood considers herself to have been a very shy young person, but she persevered with her dreams, which could not be fulfilled as circumstances seemed to have stood in her way. Karuna went on to gain her BSc by 18, but she was never able to attend pre-med school.

So, at the age of 18 we have the picture of an intelligent young woman who, being denied the ability to follow the career of her choice, stands at the threshold of life, viewing it, in all probability, with a mixture of frustration, anticipation and perhaps resignation; emotions that may well be experienced by countless thousands of young women in the developing world.

It was at this stage, when she was studying for her MSc, that her life took a completely different turn, thereby setting to nought all her half-baked plans for the future.

Karuna's family visited Delhi in order to meet old friends. Karuna had not met these people before but 'went along for the ride'. The visit coincided with a taxi drivers' strike, and this caused problems for their friends, who did not own a car and needed transport to meet their son at the airport. The young man was resident in the UK but was visiting India for a short stay. The pickup took place and Karuna met him briefly at breakfast on his first day. Looking back she confesses that she scarcely noticed him, and did not give him another thought for the next two weeks. She might have paid more attention to him if she had realized the purpose of the visit.

Some time after the breakfast meeting Karuna was surprised when the young man's mother asked her the size of her ring finger. When she enquired the reason for this request she was told that she was engaged to be married. The whole story now came out.

It transpired that her (now) fiancée had come to India in search of a bride. Although there were many British Asians from whom to chose in the London area, her husband was concerned that they might be too Westernized, too independent for his taste – he wanted a wife who had been brought up in traditional Indian ways with traditional Indian attitudes. During his two weeks in India, he had 'interviewed' a number of potential brides, but felt that none had met the specifications as well as the girl he had encountered on his first morning. His parents had spoken to Karuna's parents, and the marriage was now arranged.

Sixteen days after the announcement of the engagement Karuna and Pravin were married.

Marriage and migration

Looking back on this period, Karuna's emotions were different from those one would anticipate in a Western woman. Instead of indignation she felt elated. Although she did not know her husband at all, first impressions made her think that she could do a lot worse. What was more, this man offered her the chance to escape from a situation that she felt was restricting her from realizing her ambitions and true potential. She was going to live in London, sophisticated centre of the universe. Here was the opportunity to become a 'woman of the world'!

Within 48 hours of the wedding ceremony the dream began to fall apart. A surprise message was relayed from England. Pravin's job was in jeopardy: it was necessary for him to return to the UK immediately if it was to be saved. Because she had no visa Karuna was forced to stay behind in India. Her new bridegroom had literally disappeared into thin air!

It was in fact, six months before they were to meet again – six months in which the bureaucracy seemed to grind with impossible slowness to come up with the entry visa to Britain.

Finally the visa was granted, and here started a period of total bewilderment. She had understood that her husband was a successful businessman, and that the streets of London were paved with gold. Not so! Her husband had indeed lost his job, and now ran a corner shop with his relative. It was a small shop, of the 'open all hours' variety, situated in Thornton Heath, outer London. It sold groceries and general household goods. Karuna and her husband were to live above the shop and, horror of horrors, there were no servants!

On the first day in the shop Karuna was confronted by two additional uncomfortable truths. First of all, she could not understand English as it was spoken in the UK. This was painfully frustrating, as she could read the language perfectly – the way it was spoken in England, however, was totally alien. Secondly, she was painfully short of domestic skills. How to iron a shirt, a duty that was expected of her, was a mystery, and even commonplace functions such as making tea with tea bags had to be explained!.

The first week was not an easy time. It was a period characterized by homesickness, feelings of alienation, insecurity and of shyness of her husband, who was still largely a stranger to her.

The need to earn money was paramount, as Pravin was not fully employed and employment was hard to find. After a week, Pravin took Karuna to a branch of Brook Street Bureau to look for a job. The interviewer there asked her a simple question: 'How old are you?'. Unfortunately, the language was still incomprehensible, and Karuna left the agency unemployed and in tears. After that there seemed to be no option other than to work in the shop.

Employment

Almost three years passed, and at the age of 21 Karuna Sood found herself looking after her two young children. One thing had changed: she now understood English perfectly.

When Karuna's son was six months old, she decided to look for a 'real' job.

This time employment was far easier to come by. Her first job was as an insurance clerk, which she obtained through an employment agency (a minor triumph), but she quite quickly got bored with the menial work and moved on to the Post Office Insurance Society, where she worked as Maturity Clerk, processing death claims and becoming involved in other forms of insurance-related clerical work.

Sood's main recollections of the Post Office Insurance Society are that it was very old-fashioned and very much the epitome of civil service work: thorough, worthy, but essentially undemanding. In addition, Sood felt stuck. The work was essentially clerical, and after eight years she was forced to admit that the nature of her work and her prospects had not changed one iota, and were unlikely to do so. Looking back, she is still uncertain whether the environment did not recognize hard work and talent, whether she was not ready for advancement in an alien culture, or whether there was something about her 'alienness' that kept her static in that position for so long.

Sood increasingly found herself saying, 'There must be something more to life than this!'.

Finally, the desire for advancement won over the cautious counsel of those close to her, and she started to actively seek a new challenge. Although she was not yet clear as to the direction that the new challenge would take her, she started to read the job advertisements and eventually found something that caught her eye.

The job at Churchill Insurance

The job was advertised in *Ms London*, a free magazine aimed at clerical and secretarial staff, usually given away at commuter stations. The organization was looking for Customer Service Assistants, and the style of the advertisement was more modern, more 'zappy' than most others that she had seen. What was more, it was local, and, having moved out of the shop, the Sood family were now living in Bromley. At the interview, Sood was told that the job was in sales, and her immediate reaction was that of fright, as she had never 'sold' before. Her interviewer, however, assured her that training would be given, as the company had not officially started to operate yet.

And so, in May 1989, Karuna Sood joined the sales team of Churchill Insurance.

She was initially in a team of eight people who worked under a team leader doing telephone selling. The work was hard, demanding constant application and a thick skin, but the business was in the right place at the right time, and so was Sood. She developed a talent for the work and, as the business then did not have many staff, came to the notice of Henry Englehardt, the Sales and Marketing Director, who saw her potential and became her mentor, guiding her performance and approach. In him, Sood found a role model and consciously began to base her actions on what he might have done in the same circumstances.

In an organization that was target-driven and which recognized both success and failure, Sood was soon consistently becoming the top salesperson. She admits to thriving on the praise and recognition (as well as the incentives scheme) and also was proud to be pointed out as a success to new staff by the Chief Executive, Martin Long. In September 1989, barely three months after starting in sales, she was promoted to Assistant Team Leader and had eight people of her own to motivate.

Sood regarded this promotion as not only a further chance to shine but also a concrete opportunity to help others shine as well. Her instinctive leadership style was that of leading by example, and her approach was that of setting targets of phone rates and sales successes and then challenging the team members to beat her. In a nutshell, her approach was that of 'come on then, beat me!', but there was more to it than that: she soon became aware of the paramount need for other types of communication.

In a target-driven team, whose main function was to handle incoming calls, she felt the need for mutual encouragement and support. Every morning, there was a team briefing at which targets were discussed and set. Sood would set herself a target as well at these gatherings, and would make sure that hers was always the most demanding and that other people's reflected their experience and abilities. These morning meetings were supplemented by frequent team lunches, which had the dual function of allowing for discussion in depth and also for more subtle team bonding.

In due course, this mixture of leading from the front backed by a strong supportive approach paid off, and the whole team's performance flourished. It was perhaps because of this that Sood's activities once again came to the attention of Henry Englehardt, who posed a new challenge to her.

A step further

Karuna Sood was totally amazed when Englehardt asked her to take on the role of unofficial Sales Trainer for Churchill. Her first reaction was to protest that she had never done anything like this before and that it was well outside her experience or competence, but Englehardt replied that she did not realize her full range of talents and should be far more aware of what she could bring to the party. With these words ringing in her ears, Sood took advantage of the opportunity and agreed. Then came part two of the challenge. Having given her advice on how to structure a training session, Englehardt gave her the task of reading through the training manual on a Friday, and told her that the first training session that she would be running would be on the following Monday.

Sood remembers that weekend as one of the worst in her life. Filled with hard study and nervous anticipation, her fear was only mitigated by the fact that she knew that she was good at the subject she had been asked to train others in and by her growing confidence in the fact that if you did something well it could lead on to advancement. There was also the feeling that much of her advancement to date had been achieved through working with and through other people – here was another opportunity!

The training sessions went well, and proved to Sood that she could communicate her expertise in formal as well as informal ways. They also provided her with a model of leadership that she could work on and adapt to her own situation. At first Englehardt sat in on her sessions. He did not interfere unless she asked for his help, but made it known that he was there if she needed him. Then, as her confidence and expertise rapidly grew, he left her to it. One piece of feedback that he gave her sustained her throughout many a session: 'When I saw that you so obviously believed in what you were saying, I knew that it was safe to leave you in charge'.

The success in the training arena emboldened Sood to ask Englehardt for advancement. He suggested that she should study for the ACII qualification. She replied that it would be difficult with her family commitments, but his advice was 'Let's see what you can do'. She did – and passed with distinction. (*Delight!*)

With increased confidence, Sood reminded Englehardt of his challenge and, as good as his word, he promoted her to Sales Controller. Now she had three teams under her, and additionally had to work as part of a team with three other controllers, one of whom was her ex-boss.

As someone with a substantial leadership role (24 people) who would now be increasingly compared to other peer leaders, Sood started to look for the differentiator – the element that would be her forte. She chose the concept of *making the learning happen* as her province.

In a new organization, methods of communication were still only just emerging, and Sood seized on them as her own. If sales staff could fully appreciate the impact of their efforts, then surely they would be motivated to do more and to seek even more innovative approaches. She set herself up as the chief communicator of progress to the telephone sales floor and set out to pass on facts and figures in as inspirational way as possible. To do this it was necessary to communicate with people at all levels and because she had worked her way up through every level possible within the organization she found this comparatively easy. She could truly say, 'I've been there, I've done it. I know your problems'. Another approach she used when people complained about targets was to challenge them to 'beat management'.

Churchill used incentive schemes, and Sood found that her conversations with people about them developed her own leadership style. On the one hand she was quite prepared to challenge others by saying, 'If I can earn money under the new schemes then surely you can too', but she learned that that approach was not enough in itself. It was necessary to listen, and if the barriers of professional distance were ignored then the communication was greatly enhanced. If other people's suggestions were listened to with interest, then the need to issue orders was greatly diminished; people would own the ideas being discussed and be motivated without the need for further input from above.

Change and challenge

Henry Englehardt's influence over Karuna Sood's career both as boss and mentor had been considerable. She herself had developed theories on the importance of mentoring as a definitive leadership activity as a result. Consequently she was shocked when he announced that he was to leave Churchill to found Admiral, a new organization. There then followed an exciting, if stressful, period.

Martin Long, Chief Executive of Churchill and another person who influenced Karuna's career and for whom Sood has respect, offered her the job of Assistant Sales Manager, with a good package and about 180 sales staff reporting to her.

Her career continued apace, and in January 1992 Sood was promoted to Sales Manager, with responsibility for approximately 250 people, a number that was increasing rapidly.

This rapid progress does not mean that life was either simple or easy. In fact, as she advanced a whole new range of leadership problems and challenges began to present themselves.

The essential leadership problem facing Sood was that of credibility. To some extent it had always been with her, but now in her more senior and visible role it was magnified. When she was first promoted to Assistant Sales Manager she had found it necessary to win over the rest of the executive: colleagues found her too soft and too subservient, despite the drive and enthusiasm that she usually displayed. To what extent these were characteristics that people expected of her and were consequently ready to criticize her for, whether they were displayed or not, is uncertain. However, when she was promoted to Sales Manager the situation was exacerbated.

Some of her previous bosses were now working for her. In a nutshell, the hurdles facing her were her sex, the fact that she was 'foreign' and the fact that she was perceived as having no previous management experience. So how did she cope with all of this?

As someone who had been essentially activity-based, Sood was now forced to think quite deeply about her role and the strategy of interpersonal relationships that she would pursue to make it a success. It was vital to get the respect of the immediate team working for her as well as the team of which she was now a new member. Her reflections also drew her to conclude that many people probably felt threatened by her success, especially those over whom she had 'leapfrogged'.

An immediate strategy, therefore, was to make people feel reassured. She let it be known that managers would certainly continue to have the authority they had previously enjoyed, but with one major difference – people were going to communicate with each other more and better. By working hard on the methods of communication with her immediate team, Sood began to win the team members' confidence. At the same time, there was no abdication of authority. She let it be clearly known that the buck stopped with her, and that there were some decisions that she insisted on making and others that she insisted on being consulted about. Thus, by a combination of firmness and democracy, communicated in both meetings and actions, her legitimate authority grew. This authority was further augmented by the fact that Sood was always ready to give the reasons for her decisions and to express her views clearly.

Influence was exerted subtly through a series of informal lunches with key people, both senior and junior to her. She took special care to keep communicating with the sales team leaders as a means of ensuring that she did not get too distant from the 'coal face'. The message got round that, despite her meteoric rise, she was still the same old Karuna, even if this Karuna had to be taken rather more seriously than before.

By making a success of her immediate leadership challenge, Sood sent a strong message to her peers among the senior executives – she was to be taken seriously. And this they did.

In 1994, Sood was promoted again, this time to Senior Operations Manager. After a reorganization there were four individual divisions, and Sood was promoted to manage one of the divisions. One of four senior executives, her responsibilities now covered Sales Floor, the Customer Service Floor, the Claims Floor and Finance. She found it to be like running a small company, and the demands being made on her were different and more difficult: along with the necessity to think on a wider business platform, the politics of the position were also different and more stretching.

And this is where she was when I met her for the second time. As somebody for whom the pace of personal and professional change had progressed at lightning speed, she had matured and been moulded in the crucible of intense growth and competition. From here, she continued to mature within the role for a further year as well as adapting to further changes within Churchill. It was a further year before she told me her life's history and gave her views on the aspects of leadership that she had found to be most important to her.

Competencies and beliefs

In many respects, one of Karuna Sood's main competencies is illustrated by her life and work history: the competency of tenacity. Effective leaders need to be able to overcome adversities and to maintain application as well as energy over long periods. Being tough is much more than making a lot of noise in the workplace; it can be a silent and lonely activity. It also can mean playing the long game – so how did this affect the delicate balance between work and home life?

The Sood household is a busy one. Pravin reinstated his career long ago and now helps run a rapidly growing and very successful company specializing in telecommunications. Pravin is also very supportive in helping Karuna solve challenges by discussing and thrashing things out, but his job also involves driving prodigious distances on a daily basis. There are, of course, implications for the children in a family such as this, and Karuna has sidestepped the potential disadvantages by making a determined effort to involve her two children (a daughter named Ekta – which means 'unity' – and a son named Anmol – which means 'precious' – who are both doing really well at school) in everything she does. Work is a common topic of conversation in the home, issues are openly discussed and the children are up to date with the issues and developments that occupy their mother.

This strategy of involvement has paid high dividends. The children have taken a pride in their parents' achievements for several years. What is more, they realize their own part in the overall success. Prosperity and security are both immediate and long-term family priorities. Everyone in the family knows the demands that this strategy makes on them, but also can see the tangible benefits. In many respects it is a team effort, and Sood believes that if the family faces a demanding future as a team then it should succeed as a unit. This belief carries her through the long hours and more stressful times.

Vision

Sood's sense of vision is essentially a practical one. Not for her the world of far-out imaginings: it is more a case of 'How do we achieve what we are setting out to do?'. How, for example, do we get the sales floor to work more effectively? Being a loyal servant of the organization, she tends to look at problems from Churchill's view: how far can she take Churchill? The vision essentially is that of progress: it is not quantified or expressed in flowery rhetoric or dazzling pictures. She admits that for her vision to be more communicable to others she may have to quantify it, or express it differently.

Work and the future

In looking at the future, Sood's thoughts are essentially bound up with the future of Churchill Insurance. Being both loyal and practical, she looks ahead to what the organization might become in the future. She admits that working for Churchill has become a way of life for her, and she is intrigued by the question of how to keep *the spirit of Churchill*, the best of what there is as the organization grows and changes. For her, the future could well be seen through the expansion of the organization – new branches, Europe and expansion of services turning Churchill into a sort of Marks & Spencer of the insurance world. The nature of work and the future of the organization are inextricably bound together. For her, progress remains the driving vision. Being practical, she knows that a way will be found.

An approach to work

The foregoing does not mean that Sood is unimaginative in approach. First and foremost she is a follower of her intuition, which she regards as one of her greatest gifts. Although a follower and user of graphs, charts and figures, she is always looking beyond them and asking herself what they really mean.

Rules, however, are there to be broken. Sood is quite willing to 'bend' them according to the situation and the people involved. A tactic she is quite ready to employ in dealing with people is to say, 'If you give me what I want, I'll bend the rules for you'.

Although no anarchist, Sood regards rules as no more than useful guidelines. The main 'rule' is progress and expansion. Consequently, rules are a useful help when you are starting out on something, but after that she would expect to challenge them consistently, and regards that as the duty of any effective leader, especially when change is in the air.

Communication and facilitation

Karuna Sood gets many of her 'kicks' from the job through working with and through people. Indeed, when she has had to work alone for any period of time, her colleagues joke that she is overdue for her next 'fix' of staff communication.

As a communicator, she favours the open door policy, and this has been formalized into a series of frequent open afternoons – a time when anybody reporting to her (either directly or indirectly) can come and talk to her. These afternoons are not clinics where staff come to unburden their worries or request favours; rather, they are general chat sessions. People are free to come and talk about anything from 'promotions to curry recipes'. It is by keeping the agendas so open that Sood has avoided the potential accusation that she has somehow sidestepped the normal chains of the hierarchy in setting up this process. As a people person, she openly admits that she loves to speak to people about anything and everything, and therefore gets as least as much benefit from these meetings as do her staff.

Power and politics

If this leader has an Achilles' heel, it is in her approach to organizational politics. As she moved higher up the organization, she found it increasingly necessary to play the political game. Here she freely admits that she did less well.

She is anxious to stress that Churchill as such is not an overtly political organization, but as in all organizations, politics does exist as an active phenomenon. As someone who has valued the mentor approach – both having a mentor and being a mentor – the demands of having to change her management style to a less open approach, an approach where influence is achieved through less straightforward means, has been difficult. Sood has always wanted to be the best and for her team to be the best. New situations, where corridor politics takes a more important role and the nature of conflict is different and less open, are more difficult for her – she misses the more straightforward people side of the job.

A current development assignment in Business Development, which has temporarily moved her out of direct people management, has increased her awareness that, for her, leadership is about people; it is about interaction with them; and it is about the camaraderie of chasing targets as part of a team.

Summary and conclusions

Leaders need to have tenacity, and the tenacity may have to be displayed over a number of years as opposed to weeks or months. While luck is important on the road to success, it is the quality of tenacity that helps us to make our own luck.

In the case of Karuna Sood, other elements also prevailed. By being a good 'operator', she caught the attention of an influential mentor and sponsor, someone who believed in her and who was able to bring forces to bear on her career progress. This is something that she in turn learned and translated into her passion for dealing with and getting the most out of other people – for her communication and leading from the front became the method and indeed the main kick out of leadership. They are, however not enough. Being a leader demands a flexibility of approach that also means having to be politically adept: it is a new and different type of toughness, and one that, alas, cannot be taught.

Finding the right political position and maintaining it is a skill that effective leaders must develop. It is a necessary, if possibly regrettable, part of their maturation as leaders. It is a skill with which Karuna Sood, at the time of writing, is currently wrestling.

Key strengths and portable qualities

- Developed a sense of purpose around a need to fulfil her own potential.
- Ability to recognize a role model and to base own ambitions around the example given by that person.
- Determination to rise to the challenges, even when intimidated by them.
- Able to empathize with people at all levels.
- Sees need to work on and reinforce her credibility and personal authority in the role of leadership.
- Determination to balance work and home life. Ability to see own family as a team.

David Venn
Leader and controller of risks

CHAPTER 4

David Venn works out of an anonymous looking office in central London. It is placed strategically midway between the houses of Parliament and Victoria Station, and tourists and commuters pass by outside without stopping to think about what goes on beyond the unassuming entrance. However, the building houses Control Risks – an organization that is totally different from the norm; an organization that exists because other organizations frequently run into trouble or experience crises which are totally beyond their experience or capacity to solve.

Within Control Risks, Venn's office is tiny and unassuming. This does not bother him, as the trappings of power and status have long ceased to impress him. On a more practical note, he is seldom in it often enough to be concerned about it. If you were to pass David Venn in the street or to meet him casually you probably would not think twice about him. In his early fifties, David Venn is tall, slim and at first sight unremarkable. Although unassuming by nature, he is outgoing and has a ready sense of humour. It is only when you get to know him better that you begin to detect the steel core that underpins this (perhaps deliberately?) unexceptional exterior.

When asked who he is and what he does, Venn's casual response is that he is an ex-soldier who, on retiring from the army, now holds a middle management position. The reality behind this throw-away statement is that until very recently Venn was General Manager of Response for the Control Risks Group. The group is an 'international specialist management consultancy providing political risk assessment, crisis management, investigative and security management services to corporations governments and private clients'. It is the world leader in risk assessment, crisis management and international problem-solving. In other words, when you are thinking about the unthinkable, or the unthinkable happens to you – call Control Risks.

As Managing Director of Response, Venn's job has been to head a team of consultants who are made available if a company falls victim to a crisis, such as kidnap, product contamination or political hostage-taking. His division specializes in advice to organizations faced with hostage-taking or detention worldwide. As a result, the work includes liaison with national agencies, diplomatic representatives, law enforcement organizations, military forces and top-level corporate managers. As a high proportion of the crises fall into the category of 'kidnap', much of Venn's work is directly concerned with securing the release of the victims, and as Control Risks do not believe in non-operational directors, Venn finds himself actively involved.

The context

Established in 1975, the business philosophy of Control Risks (CR) is that many aspects of risk in the pursuit of business or commercial venture cannot be covered fully by normal mechanisms. A variety of incidents can befall a well-meaning organization, and even though an incident may appear drastic at the time, its effects may have impacts far beyond the immediate consequences. The poor handling of a crisis may have a lasting impact on a company's reputation and be subject to close scrutiny by the law, its employees, the media and its shareholders.

Although its services are confidential in nature, Control Risks has established a unique reputation for helping organizations cope with the unthinkable and the unimaginable. If your Chief Executive is kidnapped while on a business trip to Columbia, if you receive a call stating that large quantities of your retail food has been deliberately poisoned, or if you discover that you are vulnerable to large-scale fraud – it is a case of call in Control Risks.

In the 20 years since its inauguration, Control Risks has worked with over 2000 clients in over 100 countries. It now has a network of offices in London, Amsterdam, Frankfurt, Paris, Moscow, Mexico City, Washington, Bogotá, Tokyo, Melbourne, Manila and Singapore, as well as significant contacts in many other countries. Its brochures list its main activities as covering (among other things) the following areas:

- Personal security
- Business disruption
- Risk analysis and surveys
- Security engineering
- Intellectual property protection
- Fraud vulnerability
- Personal vetting and pre-employment screening

A key activity is that of 'response', and it is this area that has been Venn's responsibility.

In order to provide the speed of service that is necessary to help organizations that are facing something completely new, CR maintains a team of consultants who are made immediately available to assist a company if it falls victim to a crisis. To date, these consultants have spent over 17 000 days advising clients in crisis. Almost all of these incidents have meant travel, with CR guaranteeing a 24-hour response to a call for help. As 31% of these cases have been in Latin America, 39% in Europe and 13% in Africa and the Middle East, with the remaining 17% predominantly being in North America, South-East Asia and Australia, this has meant a phenomenal amount of travel for Venn and his team. When they are not on a case they will be studying other cases, as understanding the motivation and tactics of criminals and members of extremist groups enables them to anticipate the likely turn of events.

So the life of a member of the response group is likely to be tough. The demands of the job can appear unreasonable. The amount of notice the organization gives before response and action is required is usually zero, and the amount of travel can be punitive, with the situations they face on arrival being highly stress-laden and often emotional. In addition, they are expected to impose order on a situation that may be perceived to be totally out of hand and to deal with people who act upon a completely different set of rules; that is, if they recognize any rules whatsoever.

Venn stresses that the nature of the service is advisory, and that he is in no way a sort of James Bond being sent in to rescue the hapless kidnap victim. (Indeed, he states unequivocally that the worst thing that can happen to you once you have been kidnapped, apart from the actual fact that you *have* been kidnapped, is for somebody to try to rescue you. You are in far greater danger from a group of would-be rescuers who may not be able to distinguish captor from victim, than from the kidnappers themselves, for whom you represent an asset.) It does, however, take a very special sort of person to do the sort of work undertaken by his team. Neither a rescue agent nor hostage negotiator, his job is to bring about a successful outcome in situations of duress. It is a difficult and demanding form of leadership, and it requires both a certain approach as well as a certain sort of individual.

Consequently, it is especially useful to look at David Venn's background at this point, as well as to hypothesize that, although the type of work that he does is well outside the normal, the variety of approaches that he successfully adopts may become much more the norm for business leaders in general as we move towards a time of increasing speed of change, when the definition of what is normal or reasonable is more frequently and persistently challenged.

Background and influences

Much of Venn's working life has been as a career soldier, having joined the army straight from school in 1961. As he says, soldiering was what he had always wanted to do, and so at the first opportunity he did it.

The 30 years that followed gave Venn a varied and extremely cosmopolitan experience. As he puts it, 'the army never let you stay put for more than a couple of years. They will move you on and give you an extraordinary range of jobs, all of which they will expect you to master'.

Having been commissioned into the Intelligence Corps, Venn subsequently served in the Parachute Regiment, The Royal Marines Commando Brigade and the Sultan of Oman's Forces during the Dophar War. He was also involved in four separate counter-insurgency campaigns world-wide. These different and varied postings gave him different experiences of leadership and also earned him four citations for distinguished service.

Other postings which he looks back on with affection were to the UN in Cyprus and to the International Military Staff at NATO Headquarters in Brussels. He states with some modesty that a knowledge of French, Spanish, German and Turkish has helped his career, and adds with some understatement that the year he spent in Istanbul learning the language was great fun and a mind-broadening experience.

Experience of a more formal and academic nature was acquired at The British Army Staff College, The Nato Defence College and The Canadian National Defence College. Venn asserts with pride that he is a graduate of these establishments and stresses, in his view, the importance of the merging of formal learning with practical experience to create the rounded and effective officer. He also thinks that the armed forces tend to balance this mixture more correctly than many industrial and commercial counterparts.

In 1991 Venn held the rank of Brigadier General, and with six years to go before reaching retirement age it was clear that further promotions were possible. At this stage, however, he made what might appear to be quite a strange decision. Instead of opting to stay in service and aspiring to be 'the very model of a modern Major General', he took a positive decision to retire. The motivation behind this decision was complex, but the key factor centred on the level of challenge that the contrasting options in his life now held out for him. If he were to stay in the army, the future to all intents and purposes would be predictable – opportunities for active operational service would be much reduced, and the bureaucratic life of a senior officer held less attraction. Furthermore, he had been in contact with Control Risks since its inception in 1975, and in the time frame that he had given himself for making the decision to leave the army, an 'appropriate slot' had become available. Based on his curriculum vitae, he was offered what he describes as the 'middle management' post of General Manager of the Response Division.

A notable characteristic of David Venn is that he tends to underplay his achievements with disarming modesty, underpinned with a sly sense of humour and throw-away remarks, most of which are highly amusing. On one point, however, he is adamant. The sort of work undertaken by him and his team can only be done by a minute percentage of the population. Venn's previous experience was *critical* in landing him the job, because of his exposure to both a wide geographical and cultural spread and to a range of life-threatening and hazardous circumstances requiring immediate response without consultation.

Since arriving at Control Risks, Venn has personally advised on kidnap cases in the Philippines, Colombia, Angola, Burma (Myanmar), Ecuador, Niger, Brazil, Zaire and Guatemala. Despite his assertion that only people with a certain background can perform his role, he is certain that the form of leadership that he uses when on assignment is relevant to more normal circumstances where the unreasonable may be taking place, even if the context is not life-threatening, and that it can be applied as a model of team leadership that embraces many modern techniques. He also believes that the view of leadership taught to him by the army and since practised on many occasions has not only helped him at Control Risks but is also relevant and useful to civilian circumstances.

The army: lessons of leadership

Although he got out early, Venn considers that the army is the finest training ground for leadership and that it has much to teach the civilian world about it. It is worth noting that the forces have been training people specifically for leadership for centuries, while the concept of leadership development in business is, in comparison, almost brand new.

Venn is grateful to the army, principally because it considers that leadership *can* be taught. While it does not enter into the philosophical debate as to whether leaders are born or made, it does look for leadership *potential* in its recruits and then considers that, whatever leadership characteristics they may be showing, those characteristics can be developed and improved on.

A crucial lesson about the nature of leadership that Venn learned with the army was that there is no single element that defines somebody as a leader. Rank alone certainly does not bestow leadership, and the supposition that it does has led to the demise of many an aspiring officer.

So, what does bestow leadership in the armed forces?

The process of development from raw trainee to Second Lieutenant, states Venn, is a tough one: the aspiring officer has to do things better than everyone else and fewer allowances are made along the way. So, when young officers emerge, everybody knows that they have 'survived the wringer' – they have already proved certain things about themselves and so have basic credibility. It is, however, more than that. Venn considers that it is the complex interaction of human characteristics and the situation in hand that leads to the emergence of leadership.

In explanation of this, Venn cites the example of new officers who are empowered at a very young age and *for real*. For them, empowerment means that they have genuine control of a group of men whom they might have to lead through hazardous, or even life-threatening situations. Consequently, they have to pick up some key techniques and learn to use them quickly. What are they? 'Well, for a start', states Venn, 'listen to your platoon sergeants; they want to help'. An early lesson for new leaders, he considers, is learning how to take advice and act on it. Venn can remember the names of each of his platoon sergeants ('They were teaching me without formally teaching me. The respectful word of guidance, the fact that they were proud of the number of officers that they had helped succeed'), whereas he has forgotten the name of many a brother officer.

Another lesson about leadership that the army continually emphasizes is its rolling nature. There is always something to learn, and the fact that the officer will advance through the ranks means that adjustments to the *style* of leadership are required from time to time.

Then there is the concept of accountability, there is no escape from the decisions you make. The realization that there is no real leadership without accountability is quickly driven home. However, the army will tell you where you are going wrong, says Venn. Guidance is systematic, and as a young officer you are helped by being shown the reports that cover both your successes and failures. How many young people in the world of business have the benefit of this type of feedback – sometimes painful, but always useful?

Formative events and reflections

Although he has seen action, it is not the combat situations that most readily spring to mind when Venn talks about the events and situations that most formed his views about leadership. After all, when you are in combat you are putting into practice everything that you have been trained to do, and if your leadership has been good to date, you know implicitly that you will be followed.

Paradoxically, it is his time on selection boards, selecting the next generation of leaders, that made the greatest impression on him. He sat on his first board when he was a Colonel. The board consisted of five officers of similar rank and two staff who spent two days together selecting from a list of 200 candidates. This meant reading all the reports on them, and, as they had been told specifically what to look for, clarity came. The members of the board agreed on their choices in the vast majority of cases, and, where they did not, vigorous debate soon brought about consensus.

Visitors from the private sector who viewed one of the boards said that their companies could not afford such an elaborate and costly system, and it was then that Venn realized that the selection of leaders was a vital part of leadership itself. The system was good and worked; it was part of the management job. However, the actual act of selection and the subsequent development was a vital element of leadership.

Failure, praise and respect

Where there is selection there is inevitably failure, and Venn considers that he learned a great deal from observing the failures of other people – both in terms of selection boards and in other venues. Why did they fail? What can be personally learned from their failures? The most telling lesson he considers to be learned is from the example of those who think that they are good but still fail. Have they deluded themselves? Have they grown arrogant and distanced themselves from reality? Whatever the reason may be, Venn feels that there is a lot to be learned from these people. Try to find the cause of their failure – and then *don't* do likewise!

When it comes to measuring success, Venn thinks that one of the best yardsticks is the unsolicited praise of your peers. In the army you have to force the boss to be good – your life may depend on it – so that when you are doing well the positive feedback comes in order to reinforce the behaviour. The army generates a mutual respect and mutual interest through which the leader and the led communicate and which greatly aids operations. He considers that this is another major lesson that the army can offer to civilian operations.

When it comes to mutual respect, Venn's observation tells him that this is lacking in the private sector. He has seen a number of instances of people 'chucking their weight around', of yuppies and others having major ego trips. In the army, you have proved that you are good and are continually retested, so there is less need for rules and regulations to be used as a blunt instrument – this approach is for use only as a last resort.

A truism that he considers the army taught him is that the led actually seek leadership! Unfortunately, the led do not always get the quality leadership that they seek.

So, when David Venn left the army he had a wealth of experiences of and thoughts about leadership to apply to this most unusual civilian job. What exactly does it involve and what forms of leadership are now demanded of him?

The job

As General Manager of Response, David Venn is in control of a team of 10 consultants (mostly male, although more than one consultant slot has been successfully filled by a woman). Like him, these people are all now in their second careers, with successful previous professional lives, mostly in the armed forces, police force or other branches of government service, behind them.

Although the team members are all individuals and sometimes strongly individualistic, there are common threads in both their background and current work that binds them together. They have all come from backgrounds that have required something beyond the norm from them, they have all been leaders in the past and they all implicitly understand that their current roles place them in situations that require leadership from them and leadership talents which, albeit in unusual contexts, could be very much the talents and actions that will increasingly be required of other leaders, though in more normal contexts.

The core activity is to arrive anywhere in the world where the *advisory* services of Control Risks have been requested within 24 hours of a kidnapping or hostage-taking having taken place. It is important to emphasize the advisory nature of the response, as the job is not to be a hostage negotiator with the kidnappers nor in any way to lead rescue missions. There will frequently be two contrasting but linked levels of consultancy advice required:

1. Consultancy at CEO or Company President level for policy decisions in a highly developed base (for example, Western Europe or Japan).
2. Operational advice in a conflict zone in an area often lacking a good communications infrastructure or well-established law enforcement structure.

All of the Response consultants must be able to operate in either of the situations described above. One common characteristic of both is that those involved are unlikely to possess previous corporate experience on which to draw. However experienced the management team may be, they will have had no exposure to this sort of situation. So, given these circumstances, even the most mature and experienced business leaders may be reduced to acting without their customary poise. It is the crisis, along with the lack of exposure to this form of crisis, that gives rise to the need for leadership qualities within the Response consultant, and it is interesting to note that those who have overtly engaged the consultant for advice often quickly turn to that person for leadership.

Venn stresses that, in his opinion, there are two forms of leadership. One is of the 'follow me, lads' variety, and this is definitely not what is required here. What *is* needed is for the consultant to be able to help those involved, whether they be company directors or the victim's family members, to put the situation into proportion, thereby allowing the firm's management structure to progress and control the situation. Essentially, the situation is an aberration, and outside the confines of what the corporation would normally understand as a commercial crisis (for example, a serious frost in the fruit industry or a major oil spill in the oil sector). Crisis management procedures for these well-understood events do not necessarily fit the hostage scenario. It is part of the consultant's job to take the corporate team inside a totally new context. This process of defining and enabling a proper context for the situation to emerge is a complex and demanding form of leadership. But what competencies does it demand?

First and foremost, states Venn, you have to get them listening to you. This is not always as simple as it sounds, as the clients are confused, distressed and looking for quick solutions. Usually the client has set up a team of people to attack the crisis, and the Response consultant quickly has to assess whether the team is the right one for the circumstances, whether the people on it need changing and how to work with the key players on it. So, to get their attention, it is necessary to display knowledge of their sort of problem and a keen understanding of what they are going through. For example, the ability to typecast the form of aberration they are experiencing (this looks like an X kidnap) does help those involved to see it in the form of a manageable problem. This leads to an initial credibility which is augmented when the consultant indicates that the knowledge he or she brings to the situation can be implemented to produce results.

Of course, the consultant's background, his or her experience in hazardous or life-threatening situations beyond those of the group, is a key to gaining the first level of credibility, but it is soon necessary to move the group back into the current situation (their frame of reference) and to move the process further on. Another key bastion of the consultant's credibility is his or her ability to manage groups that are in stress or confusion. However, this skill is something that is to be demonstrated rather than discussed.

Even when the initial credibility has been gained the role remains demanding. Although the consultant's personal safety is seldom at risk, the job requires concentration, empathy and flexibility for every minute of the day. Decisions must be made on incomplete information and in public – there is a very focused audience for each decision and immediate accountability for its results. In addition, as a leader within the situation, the consultant controls nothing, and often has to work with the apparently unreasonable demands of both his own and the other side. So how does the consultant survive?

Venn describes himself as a loner. The job may require him to be alone in an unfamiliar part of the world working in stressed conditions for three weeks at a time. The ability to be aggressive, as well as a love of challenge, helps him through, but more than this is the ability to work with others to produce workable options. In the end, the client, having fully explored the situation with Venn's help, will say, 'Yes, I understand. But what shall we do?'. Of course, at that stage Venn answers the request for his decision-making capability by stepping into a decisive, authoritative mind set. However, the pre-work will have been done prior to that point.

Two essential elements of the pre-work are to demonstrate a businesslike approach and a fundamental integrity.

Even in the most extreme situations, people want to know all the angles. The scenario may be hazardous and it may be unreasonable, but if it can be demonstrated to be operating within perceived *business norms and restraints* then a helpful degree of structure, even if not normality, can be brought to the proceedings. Venn considers that there is a myth that ex-military people do not understand the bottom line. This, he states, is untrue, and has been for some years. In general, they understand the need to be commercial and how to use resources. Leaders, whatever the situation, must be businesslike.

Integrity is a fundamental part of the consultant's credibility. It has to be beyond question, as the consultant must become speedily absorbed into either the business's task force or the family. Indeed, the friendships that he has struck up have often been close and long-lasting. It is the integrity that can move the consultant's statements from 'I am here to help you' to 'I am here to guide our individual responses back into well-understood management responses'. It is then that clients start to emerge from their panic and muddle and start to see a way forward. Venn considers it impossible to overstress the importance of personal integrity in his line of work. It is the cornerstone of his credibility with the client, and this credibility has to be passed on from one consultant to another. Control Risks does not allow its people to work on location on a case for more than three weeks without a break, so many cases are passed from one consultant to another and then back again. Control Risks deploys a team of two as a matter of course, so that there is also continuity of personality in long-lasting cases. Each consultant's credibility must be beyond question, and the credibility must be passed from one to another along with the case notes.

In helping a group to address the crisis in a cohesive and businesslike way, Venn accepts that a large part of his role is that of a facilitator, but a flexible facilitator who is able to judge the nature of his behaviour to meet unreasonable demands and extraordinary situations.

The lessons for 'normal' business leaders

A common feature of many good leaders is that they invest time to think about their role as leaders. Here Venn is no exception, and from his point of view the most transferable features are clear, if not always what you would expect, and are talents that he has worked on and honed both in the army and in Control Risks.

They can be summarized as follows:

- Sensitivity to interactions
- Handling of uncertainty and dilemmas
- Ability to work with teams
- Ability to think intuitively as well as logically
- Ability to handle conflict and stress

Sensitivity to interactions

The ability to analyse and understand the interaction of the key players in a situation is vital. Moreover, the understanding needs to be arrived at quickly. To reach this understanding, consultants must be observant: listening skills come to the fore. Once the understanding is reached, consultants must choose the behaviour needed to bring about an effective problem-solving unit; the interaction between the leaders and the led is a two-way process, and they must choose how they will make the best of the situation. Having now observed a large number of commercial organizations under pressure, Venn reckons that some company cultures are at least as hierarchical and overtly rank conscious as the army!

Handling of uncertainty and dilemmas

Much has been written of the impact of high levels of change in current business life with its accompanying rise in the level of uncertainty and unpredictability for all concerned. Venn says that his job is to act as a 'fly-in' facilitator to those for whom the pace of change has accelerated beyond all imagination and who are now facing dilemmas that have teeth like a tiger.

As a leader, Venn has to adopt a perspective that says 'Think the unthinkable!' and accept that 'Everything is imaginable!'. Too often in life people shy away from the unpleasant by saying 'Don't even think about that!'. Venn's philosophy is that 'You *must* think about it for by doing so you prepare yourself!'. It helps here, states Venn, to have a high level of intellectual curiosity and to be prepared to ponder the circumstances by which a terrorist group could tie up a society or, for example, the circumstances in which the USA might go to war with Mexico. 'It's no good saying "heaven forbid"', he says. 'Think about it!'.

It is the mental rigour and toughness that comes out of thinking the unthinkable that leads to the ability to handle uncertainty and dilemmas as well as sometimes to predict the circumstances that lead to the dilemma before it actually occurs. Venn's definition of this mental process is 'scenario thinking'. When working with the family or colleagues of the kidnap victim he obliges them to think through the situation and its implications. The very process of doing so, although uncomfortable, puts more knowledge into the situation and helps to define the uncertainty itself, thereby pointing the way to the initial responses.

Ability to work with teams

'A collection of individuals with mutually supportive skills' is Venn's definition of a team. To this I would add the phrase 'with a common purpose', but perhaps this is just too obvious for him to merit a mention.

In practice, Venn is called to work with teams under two circumstances, each one making different demands on him. The first is the interaction with the crisis management team that he will have arrived to join and assist. The second circumstance is his ongoing relationship with his team of Response consultants.

The relationships with the members of crisis teams are dynamic and interesting. When he enters the team he is a stranger – a foreigner – and the other team members are already at a high level of stress. Consequently, on arrival he often has to act as a form of lightning conductor – initially he can be the focal point for all the anger, frustration and helplessness that is being felt, and he must absorb it all before order can be found and progress made. This requires a great deal of patience and the ability to listen to and accept the vast range of emotions before exercising his influence too strongly on proceedings.

A common feature of some teams is their reluctance to take initiatives; members just do not know how to respond, and the consequences of a poor response are just too horrible to contemplate. In addition, such people are often used to having a high level of personal power and to making high-level decisions, and consequently the degree of pure frustration will be astronomic. The real job for Venn in these circumstances is to guide the structure of the meetings, to assert his credibility to deal with the situation and then to pull together the local knowledge of the members to enable a fuller understanding of the situation and the various options open to them. Very often, after the initial phase close relationships form as the team works to bring about the victim's release. During the process there will inevitably be ups and downs and hopes will rise only to be frustrated; however, states Venn, in the vast majority of kidnap and hostage scenarios the victim is released, although often after months (rather than weeks) of work and negotiation. Consequently, when the ordeal is finally over the team will be very close and, Venn adds with pleasure, many ex-team members are now close personal friends.

The relationship with his team of Response consultants is very different. Venn has management responsibilities within Control Risks, and these apply even when he is operating in the most remote outposts of Africa or South America.

The main problem is that Venn often goes for considerable periods of time without seeing some of his team members, and never manages to get the whole team together for a general meeting. So how does he cope?

A number of elements work in Venn's favour here. First of all, he is complimentary about the people in his team: they are all mature and are able to take high levels of individual responsibility. The consultants are used to operating alone and being self-reliant – that is the nature of the job, and a team of that sort does not require over-managing. The managing that does apply, whether it be planning or dealing with appraisals, applies even when he is operational, and Venn has to switch mind sets from the intense involvement with a particular case to more dispassionate management from his hotel room, where he has the tools and technology to convert it into an efficient office.

Ability to think intuitively as well as logically

For David Venn, the balance of different types of thinking processes is vital.

Often he brings some order to a confused and frightened crisis team through the forthright use of logic. He may state, 'X is a valuable commodity to the kidnappers and you do not damage valuable goods, do you?', or state 'We are now in a business situation, and in business neither side realistically expects the deal to be completed in the first round'.

On the other hand, as a professional soldier he has learned to use his intuition and to transfer it to his civilian role. A particular situation when this sixth sense was called to the fore was during a hostage-taking in Angola. In this instance an elderly European businessman had been taken hostage by rebel forces and had been transported up-country by the rebels. Venn was brought in to help advise on how to bring about his release, and in this case the work meant 400 miles of travel towards the rebel stronghold.

Various communications and negotiations brought Venn and the crisis management team who he was advising to a river that formed the natural boundary between zones. The hostage-takers and hostage were on the other bank, with Venn and team on the other, still in Angola. At this stage events took a different turn. Usually the amount of face-to-face dialogue is limited, but now the rebels demanded that Venn cross the river to the rebel camp in order to continue and hopefully conclude the negotiations. Venn was presented with a dilemma: if he did not cross the river, the hostage (who was by now weak and ill after months of captivity in the jungle) would be consigned to a further debilitating period of incarceration. If he did cross over, then there was a very real danger that he would be kidnapped as well, and logically this would be a good deal for the kidnappers – exchange a sick elderly man who might die on them for a younger stronger man for whom they could still bargain. He describes being kidnapped as 'the ultimate participant sport', and he did not want to take part.

Personal decision-making in Venn's profession is vital, and the rules by which he makes decisions may well become the norm for others in the future. His method is to break down the problem into its components, attack each bit separately, then look at the whole and drive towards a solution, while remembering that whatever rules you may think apply might change within 30 seconds. It is important not to think of anything having a middle or an end – there is just a continuum, and you must be ready for all eventualities along that continuum. You can then break a situation down into the occasions where you may 'smell danger' and act accordingly, but then return to objective judgement as soon as possible thereafter.

Venn's thought process went as follows:

> 'We have come 400 miles and they have had opportunities to do something before now but have not, so, logically, why should they try something now? If they were going to kill us they have had better opportunities. More importantly, my guts tell me that for the time being we're OK.'
>
> *Logic*: 'If I don't go over, the hostage remains a hostage.'
>
> *Intuition* (as he prepared to cross the river): 'I think that the situation is 70/30; OK, those sound good enough odds.'
>
> *Self-comfort* (as he left his territory): 'Why would they want me? They already have "our friend".'

Nevertheless, as they crossed the river Venn found himself looking at the banks for possible hiding places and escape routes should the situation get out of hand.

It so happened that Venn's intuition was right. He was safe and "our friend" was duly released. However, there was one angle that his intuition had not helped him foresee: the reason the rebels were so keen for him to have crossed over was that they had a full military parade assembled for him, as a British General, to inspect, so he had to review the ramshackle army before the 'deal' could be concluded.

Ability to handle conflict and stress

Venn is a pragmatist, with views that have been shaped by a life that has made very special demands on him. He admits that he can be contentious and that he is not afraid of conflict if it can help straighten out a situation. Consequently, as members of his response team all have firm views and strong characters, opinions can be forcibly put and the arguments fierce. However, although he enjoys a good argument, Venn does not regard himself as overtly political, and looks to conflict as a means of structuring and defining situations. Consequently it can be useful, but should not be used for its own sake or to enforce rank or personal power – something he has seen happen more often in other paths of business life.

Being a pragmatist, Venn looks at features of the business world and takes only what he sees as useful. Asked about visions in business he replies that these are fine for those who are paid to look into the future, but that his Division's whole purpose is to be reactive. As he and his team cannot influence the level of kidnapping that takes place in the world, why bother with visions?

The way that he copes with the level of stress that he faces, however, is something he can influence, and he recognizes that this is something he must do. When asked about stress his initial answer is that he is used to it. Later he will open up and reflect that a good sense of humour and strong sense of irony also help. 'Laugh about awful journeys and unreasonable delays', he says, 'especially afterwards; it helps you to get over them'. Over and above this lighthearted approach, he has a bolt-hole well out of London, where he and his wife escape either during or after the most demanding of assignments. However, there is always the telephone and the Control Risks 24-hour pledge

Summary and conclusions

It may sound strange to be looking for leadership competencies in someone who primarily claims to be a consultant. However, this particular consultant has spent most of his life as a front-line leader, and was specifically trained for it. He now uses more traditional as well as modern leadership skills to help groups who are stressed and in high-pressure situations. In doing so, could he be illustrating at least some of the competencies or activities that will be in ever-increasing demand in the future? The methods he uses when the pressure is greatest tend to veer away from the 'command and control' methods towards a set of skills that help the team define and structure the situation more clearly and thereby find its way, with Venn's help, towards successful outcomes. Perhaps when the costs of failure are too appalling to contemplate, Venn's facilitative skills become more necessary and more in demand.

Key strengths and portable qualities

- Knows how to take advice – and act on it.
- Recognition that the selection of other leaders is a key part of effective leadership.
- Ability to learn by observing other people's failures.
- Defines the situation and manages the process accordingly.
- Demonstrates integrity as a fundamental part of leader's credibility.
- Makes key decisions on incomplete information when necessary.
- Acts as facilitator, and as such helps others face change and its dilemmas.
- Ability to work with teams of all sorts
- Breaks problems down into their component parts to achieve objective analysis.
- Not afraid of conflict if it helps sort things out.

Eddie Jesudason
Service leader from the tiger economies

CHAPTER 5

Introduction: the context

Much is made of the tiger economies of the Far East and South-East Asia. Often these countries are held up to Europeans as both an example of future economic activity as well as a threat.

With prodigious growth rates and ambitious building plans, these economies surge ahead, embracing a love of change and desire for the new that makes most other parts of the world seem pedestrian in comparison. There are downsides, of course; any visitor to Kuala Lumpur will remark that the city is being developed too fast and that it is sprawling into the surrounding countryside, gobbling up the environment as it goes. Singapore, on the other hand, has no countryside; it is a city state renowned for its cleanliness and efficiency – some of the efficiency having been bought at the cost of rules and regulations that seem foreign to many Europeans.

But what of the leadership within these economies? Are the leaders in middle to senior positions all that different from those in other parts of the world? Having trained many managers in South-East Asia in both management and leadership, I found more similarities in approach and attitude than differences. Or was there something about these people being more positive and optimistic than their European counterparts? With these thoughts in mind, it was interesting to hear the in-depth views of a senior Singaporean, all the more so because he represents possibly the best known of all of Singapore's businesses.

Singapore Airlines (SIA) ranks amongst the world's foremost airlines. For years it has mounted a seductive advertising campaign based not only on discovering the mysteries of the East but also on the excellence of its service to passengers: 'Singapore girl truly is a great way to fly!'. I was consequently fortunate to get the thoughts on leadership of J. Edward Jesudason, Director of Cabin Crew for SIA, and would like to thank my Singaporean colleague, Daryll Wee, for making the contact and his help with this chapter.

The person

Edward Jesudason was born in 1939 and is known to his friends as Eddie. With an Indian father and Chinese mother, he in many respects epitomizes both the richness of racial diversity as well as the energy of South-East Asia. With a Japanese spouse and one daughter, he is an avid golfer, currently playing off a single-digit handicap. At Christmas-time he takes the family skiing. Not surprisingly he looks fit, but at the same time distinguished, with white hair and a patriarchal air that is appropriate to the culture in which he is based.

Although he has spent most of his working life with Singapore Airlines, Jesudason's first job on leaving the National University of Singapore was with a public sector trade union, where he stayed for over two years conducting research and participating in negotiations. Although he was soon to move from 'poacher to gamekeeper' by taking his first management position with what was then known as Malaya Singapore Airlines, this period was useful. 'The job exposed me to a variety of people in the workforce', states Jesudason, 'which made me familiar with many employee problems, from those of Watchmen to Nurses'.

As Assistant Personnel Superintendent, Jesudason's responsibilities were to look after matters connected with pilots – the heart of the organization – and he was later sent to Kota Kinabalu in East Malaysia to look after administration for the airline there as well as pilot relations. In a job that initially involved a great deal of travel, he returned to Singapore in 1969 and was promoted to Personnel Superintendent of Paya Lebar Airport, which was then the state's main international airport.

Following further career moves within the personnel function, Jesudason made the move into General Management when he was promoted to Manager, Thailand, in 1974. This now meant that he controlled all of the airline's operations in that country, from marketing to airport operations. The move into General Management must have suited Jesudason, as further career moves followed in swift succession, taking him from Thailand to Japan, where he ended up as Area Manager, from there back to Singapore as Area Manager, and then to the USA in 1982, from where his responsibilities covered the eastern USA and Latin America.

By 1987, Jesudason was the Regional Director, South-West Pacific, a position that moved him to Sydney in 1989 as Senior Vice-President, South-West Pacific. From Sydney, he moved back to Singapore as Director of Cabin Crew, a position that he expects to hold for approximately five years.

Looking back on a career that has involved frequent moves upwards as well as more geographical moves than the average diplomat, Jesudason reflects that the real lessons for him have been connected with people. Looking back over the years of leading people in a variety of cultures, he states that 'the main learning experience was in finding the way to deal with people of all ranks – this involved developing the ability to communicate at all levels in order to gain their confidence'. Learning to listen was both his focus and his challenge: 'the art was to listen and to find out the true reasons why a person is asking for something. This requires listening with an open mind, which is essential'.

Throughout the interview, Jesudason maintained both his business and his people focus. The way that he had dealt with people had obviously occupied his thoughts to a large extent, and his main means of expression tended to be 'we' rather than 'I'.

Context of the current role

The main purpose and objective of Jesudason's current role is to ensure that the airline is able to provide cabin crew service that is better than all the other competing airlines. This purpose dovetails neatly into the core values of the airline, which centre on service and the attainment of excellence in all things.

Core values

1. *Pursuit of excellence*

   We strive for the highest professional standards in our work and aim to be the best in everything we do.

2. *Safety*

   We regard safety as an essential part of all our operations. We maintain our equipment and adopt practices that promote the safety of our customers and staff.

3. *Customer first*

   Our customers are foremost in our minds all the time. We go the extra mile to exceed their expectations.

4. *Concern for staff*

   We value our staff and care for their well-being. We treat them with respect and dignity and seek to provide them with appropriate training and development so that they can lead fulfilling careers.

5. *Integrity*

   We strive for fairness in all our business and working relationships

6. *Teamwork*

   We work as a worldwide team to achieve success together.

Perhaps more than in any other business area, Jesudason's leadership style has a direct impact on the attainment of these core values. Most importantly, the impact of these values is felt most in the aircraft and by the passengers. Not surprisingly, he is passionate about the attainment of excellence in the work of his cabin crews: 'what makes the organization so special is that we subscribe to our own core values; therefore when we talk about the pursuit of excellence, we do not just talk about it, we live it to the core'.

The alignment of all people with the core values assists them to talk the same language and consequently provides coordination and continuity to the organization. Jesudason has a personal belief that the customer truly must come first, and that if the airline is not customer-driven it is nothing at all. In reality, there is an interesting synergy between Jesudason's values, his role, his people and the organization itself. The whole airline subscribes to the values, which are reflected back with interest by the Cabin Crew function and consequently reinforced on a company-wide basis. It is not surprising, therefore, that Jesudason sees the main challenges of his role as aligning 100% with the values.

He states the challenges concisely as:

- Providing a professional level of service, not just warmth. Therefore there needs to be a balance of soft and hard skills for cabin crew.
- Meeting the rising expectations of passengers. ('It is not good enough to do what we are currently doing. We need to always anticipate the needs of our passengers so that we can exceed their expectations'.)

As the majority of those working for Jesudason are not only thousands of miles away from him but probably also some 30 000 feet above him, the pursuit of the challenges can at best only be done by the most sophisticated methods of influence and leadership, both by delegation as well as by himself at a distance. So how has he set out to achieve his goals, and what has he achieved to date?

Influence and achievements

In any service business, progress can only be achieved by having a positive impact upon the mind sets of those providing a service right at the front line. This is even more the case with an airline, where the customer experiences the service more intensely and for longer periods of time than is the case with most other service businesses. Passengers who have flown the long hop between London and Singapore in economy class will know the truth of this. What is more, if you do not like the service in a restaurant it is always possible to leave it – if you have another ten hours' flying time you are stuck; that is, until you next have a choice of airline. So having an impact on the minds and actions of his cabin crew has been a further major challenge for Jesudason.

Achieving this level of influence has not always been easy. SIA is constantly taking on trainees to meet operational requirements and growth, and this has caused a problem in that the more established staff had readily adopted the core values of service that drive the organization; however, the increasing affluence of Singaporeans in general has meant that many new joiners paradoxically have not had the same service-oriented mind set as the more mature crew. They have considered themselves the sort of people to whom service is given rather than considering themselves the providers of service.

Consequently, Jesudason has worked hard to set out the divisional goals and to ensure that all, whether they be new trainees or established staff, both know them and subscribe to them. The message he promotes is unequivocal. It is about adding special value and adding it so sincerely that the customer knows that it is being given, even if that added extra is hard to define. As far as Jesudason is concerned, it is about exceeding expectations. This is an established and perhaps overused expression, but he has gone out of his way to give meaning to it. 'To exceed', states Jesudason, 'we must try to go beyond the normal standards – we need to bring out the special something in all our staff. If we do not bring out that something extra, the crew will just become like any other crew; there will be nothing special about us. We must therefore add value, and we can only add value if the crew adds it from their own being'.

By using statements like this, Jesudason set out to challenge his crew members. He used passion as a means of communicating the message and then tried to give meaning to the message itself. In reality, the crew must give of themselves, but what does that mean? Giving of yourself is more demanding than simply being one of the smiling faces in the 'Singapore Girl' advertisements.

SIA have always had an outstanding reputation for service, and Jesudason has maintained it, although he is uncomfortable with the idea that he has personally achieved any thing. He emphasizes that all achievements (as recognized in SIA's awards lists) were reached as a team rather than as individuals. Getting there as a team, however, was work-intensive for him as well as the team itself. It involved trust and constant repetition of the core messages. Jesudason feels that it is vital for people to believe in the goals and objectives of the division, thereby improving service and performance through the training and high morale of the crew. High morale, he states, is when you can wake up after two years on the job and still feel energized. For this to happen, he is convinced that staff selection must be right; after that, it is a matter of good leadership – and for leadership to be effective, there must be a vision.

Establishing and achieving the vision

When Jesudason came to his current role, he took some time to establish a total overview of the division. After that, he looked more closely at specific areas in order to determine more closely what required attention. Along with this went the essential job of getting to know his new colleagues. His initial approach was cautious, but by establishing himself in his position by a process of examining areas of need as well as by building relationships he put himself in to a position of strength when it came to having a vision and to making changes.

As a leader, Jesudason recognized his role as a change agent, but he also acknowledged the fact that change was a risk, especially for a division that was already successful and which had a strong reputation within SIA. The dangers in being a strong visionary change agent lay in the ever-present possibility that the changes might actually result in deterioration! He did, however, acknowledge that it was necessary to take risks in order to grow and improve. With this in mind he set out to challenge the existing processes and to modernize the whole concept of cabin crew and what they did.

The vision of a 'Modernized Cabin Crew' meant that he wanted to give crew members the authority to innovate, to be different and to take positive risks in the way that they went about their work. This did not mean that they were being invited to throw the rule book out of the cabin window, but it did carry the message 'Don't worry about making mistakes if the purpose and intentions are good'. As Singapore is a society which adheres to rules far more closely (for better or worse) than the typical European society, this statement was more provocative than at first it might appear. Consequently, with it came an imperative for him to convince both crew members as well as managers that this was a policy worthy of implementation.

Both the vision and the process of persuasion that went with it were achieved through the training of those involved as well as by achieving an understanding of their views and opinions on the subject. Both of these were helped by the fact that Jesudason was prepared to spell out exactly what he meant. 'We need to allow for the flexibility to vary and be different, hence we cannot punish people for being different. However, there needs to be a balance between being flexible and being consistent in our services so that we always exceed passenger's expectations.' Underlying this statement was Jesudason's belief that the work should be fun. A sense of fun would lead to the right sort of spontaneity, as he knew that if crew positively enjoyed their jobs then everything else would fall into place. In a roundabout way, his vision for modernization would be helping his people to be more creative as well as more productive in their work.

The vision was further developed through his team by means of immediate reports. They examined what was already in place, past results and history, and then looked for areas of modification that would take them where they wanted to go. The process was one of openness, with brainstorming sessions taking place that were open to all levels. During the brainstorms, the emphasis was to *challenge existing concepts*. Jesudason used the brainstorming sessions as well as the Cabin Crew Division's Yearly Business Meetings to debate and further develop the goals and objectives springing from his original vision.

While many aspects of the vision were developed by teams, Jesudason did not hesitate to inspire others to pursue the vision. For him, being inspirational means setting an example as leader – an absolute must. To set an example it is necessary to be visible, especially with crew members who are always on the move. To attain a sufficient level of visibility therefore meant participating in as many of their activities as possible – quite a challenge for somebody who was already a busy man. At the same time, Jesudason pursued an open door policy – this helped him influence, inspire and support on a very individual basis when necessary. He considers that having a genuine open door policy enables people to get to know you. If you appear to be genuinely accessible then others will feel more comfortable with you. It will all start to work in your favour.

But for Jesudason, support for his people goes beyond having an open door policy or being a good listener. While he is a believer in staff welfare, it also means going beyond good welfare policies. Support means that the crew must be recognized, especially those who do well. SIA has traditionally given awards for excellent or outstanding cabin crew, and when Jesudason took over as Director he instituted a new team-based award which recognized teams primarily for the quality of their teamwork. With an average of 18 to a crew this constituted a significant challenge to all concerned.

Problems in attaining the vision

The main problem was resistance to the challenge that the vision implied. Interestingly, resistance did not simply stem from resistance to change itself, but mainly from those who had been in the organization for some time and had tried to change things and failed. The attitude was, 'I've tried and it didn't work. Why bother trying again?'. In addition, the long service of many people in the division, combined with limited exposure to the way that things were done elsewhere, had led to an 'if it ain't broke, don't fix it' mentality.

Jesudason overcame this sort of thinking by communicating as hard as he could. All channels of communication were opened, and this often meant that there was considerable debate over a variety of issues, as well as testing of ideas. In meetings, feedback was often candid and forthright, but Jesudason was anxious to use them as productively as possible. Rules of conduct developed, the most powerful one being that, 'You can say what you feel it is necessary to say as long as it is said without disrespect; there needs to be a balance between openness and objectiveness and then things will get done'. The net effect was to reduce the resistance to change and enabled Jesudason to pursue a policy of testing innovations on a small scale before subsequently implementing them if they were seen to be viable.

One example of such a test was in the field of discipline standards. Traditionally such standards had been very rigid in SIA, but Jesudason's vision of a modernized cabin crew allowed for the seemingly heretical concept of allowing people to make mistakes. Eventually others came to see that this provided a balance in the discipline equation that allowed for greater creativity. Standards of service and conduct still had to be followed, but now more leeway for interpretation was allowed. The result of this new approach was a visible increase in motivation among crew members, as well as an overall improvement in morale.

When asked how the achievement of his vision is measured, especially a vision that is primarily focused on behaviour rather than financial targets or other more tangible measures of business performance, Jesudason emphasizes both soft and hard measures. At one level he believes that the vision is being achieved simply through the increased number of compliments that crew members receive from passengers as well as the fact that the feedback that the crew give their managers indicates that they are substantially happier in their work. Another simple measure of the vision's successful implementation can be seen in the figures relating to sick leave, staff turnover and other measures of attrition, all of which have fallen.

Put these figures together with the increase in passenger satisfaction and it is obvious that something is going 'right' at the sharp end.

Influence, intuition and trust

Singaporean culture has a reputation of being analytical, rigid in many ways and rule-bound. This is not the sort of culture that encourages intuition or lateral thinking, and Jesudason admits that he has to be ordered in his thinking and very logical, especially when dealing with pilots and their work. On the other hand, he does use intuition in reaching many of his decisions, as most of his decision-making concerns the work of cabin crew, who constantly have to deal with people-related situations. Of course, there are standard procedures to cover a wide variety of the situations facing crew members, but as SIA expects them to use intuition, as well as considering the facts, when making judgements about the people-related situations they face, it seems only fair to use his intuition when dealing with them or making decisions about them.

In the end, Jesudason accepts that there needs to be a balance between logic and intuition – and therein lies the dilemma for many a leader. An example he cites is in the recruitment and selection of cabin crew. He considers that the selection process lies at the heart of the division's success: select the right raw material and then everything that follows will be easier. The selection process is rigorous and based on a variety of tests. The final decision on whether or not to hire a candidate, however, is based on whether the recruiters 'feel' they can do the job. The author recalls with some amusement his days working on graduate recruitment with the consultancy Ernst & Young. Monumental number-based systems were set up to evaluate candidates, but in the end it very often came down to 'gut feeling'.

Jesudason also allows his sense of intuition to play a part when it comes to exerting influence. Looking ahead, he anticipates a doubling of his staff's strength to 9000 by the year 2004. This will greatly alter the methods of communication, and although forcing through greater reliance on technology is going to be the main factor in influencing what the job is going to look like in the future, it does not preclude the power of either intuition or personal influence. Jesudason has always believed in challenging traditional mind sets and going against the organization's grain if need be.

One such instance came in a debate over dress codes. Jesudason's personal philosophy is that 'if you treat your people like adults, they will behave as adults; if you treat them like children, they will behave like children', and this philosophy led him into a very fundamental rule challenge.

SIA have always insisted on the highest levels of personal grooming for their staff. For example, the rule for female trainees was that they had to be dressed in skirt and blouse and have their hair neatly in a bun; these were the prescribed standards and people were expected to maintain them at all times throughout their careers. Jesudason decided to challenge this ruling by advocating that it should not apply to staff during their refresher training sessions and relaxed the code to the extent of (shock, horror!) allowing women to wear trousers during this training. Initially there was considerable disagreement over this from other managers, but Jesudason persisted; his view was that it was worth trying, and his line or argument was 'let's be flexible: if the idea does not work, we can easily revert to the old conventions'.

The result of implementing this quite minor change was a disproportionate increase in morale among those it affected. Many of Jesudason's immediate subordinates had disagreed with him over the change, and he had had a big selling job on his hands. Jesudason acknowledged that situations such as this are stretching for him, and that dealing with deeply held differing opinions is tough – selling ideas and being convincing also takes so much longer than simply being autocratic. In the end, however, the effort proved well worth it for the whole division and ties in with Jesudason's definition of leadership. 'The essential difference between leadership and management is that the leader inspires people to want to work. The leader is tough yet has compassion. The manager is there to carry out the task, he or she controls and implements the daily functions of the business.'

If the leader must inspire, then there cannot be true inspiration without a background of trust. Jesudason is an ardent advocate of openness, intolerant of office politics (which he will not brook within his division) and a non-believer in 'hidden agendas'. He believes that truth is essential in communication at all levels and on all matters. 'I don't believe in having hidden agendas. The truth is essential, and by sharing the truth, you can often share both your problems and your successes. If there are any hidden agendas, it is very difficult to build trust and therefore it will be very difficult to communicate.'

Jesudason accepts that there is an implied dilemma between being completely open and being over-candid with people, but he believes that the answer for the leader lies in that leader's personal sensitivity. 'I do believe in being candid; however, we also need to apply sensitivity when we are being candid. If we are able to build trust, then the fact that one is candid will be seen more as positive feedback, rather than as an attack'. However, the main means by which he both grows and demonstrates trust is through his policy on delegation.

Delegation and trust are essential steps in the development of staff in a service business. A specific example of demonstrating trust via delegation is shown in Jesudason's approach to SIA's Japan Office. Before Jesudason's intervention, a member of the Singaporean staff was required to be present when the collective staff agreement was negotiated in Japan. The final authority lay with the Singaporean. Jesudason changed the process by allowing the Japanese office staff to have full authority for the negotiations without head office supervision, thereby demonstrating his trust that they would do their best for the organization. As far as Jesudason was concerned, the benefits far outweighed the risks. He considered that small losses in terms of local benefits would be vastly offset by gaining a more committed and motivated local management who were in fact developing themselves for bigger and better things. He considers that trust, when demonstrated, leads to challenge, which in turn leads to achievement and job satisfaction.

Making the effort to achieve through communication at all levels has paid off for both the SIA and Jesudason in the past. While he was based in Australia, a baggage handler's strike virtually paralysed the airport systems. In fact, only SIA flights were able to take off or land there. Paradoxically, it was the airline's ability to communicate with its passengers that allowed its planes to fly. Passengers were told before they took off from or to Sydney that the baggage handlers were on strike. Consequently, SIA could either cancel the flight due to the fact that nobody could carry the bags and luggage to the terminal, or all those on the plane could work as a team to carry the bags. Given this choice, the passengers agreed to help out and formed a chain, along with the cabin crew, between the plane and the terminal. They then passed all the bags along the chain, with the end result that they made it to their destinations – albeit somewhat fitter and more tired than they had anticipated.

Staff and communication

As far as Eddie Jesudason is concerned, communication with the cabin crew is always the challenge and the 'stretch'. Much of the stretch comes from the challenge of trying to communicate with over 4000 people who are never in the same place at any one time and, indeed, are usually on the move. Quite obviously, it is too big a job for an individual to consider without the backup of teams as well as a variety of procedures.

Means and methods of communication with cabin crew that have been set up include training, staff functions and parties, as well as 'Check Trainers', who accompany flights to do service reviews but who also act as carriers of messages in both directions.

The baggage-handling story is in many ways a metaphor for what Jesudason wishes to achieve in terms of the atmosphere and team spirit of his staff. He is convinced that the greater the level of perceived equality, the better will be the ease of communication and subsequently of commitment at all levels. To achieve this, Jesudason has worked hard to influence the culture towards being one in which nobody flaunts their rank, nobody is made to feel inferior and everybody works as a team. This is most important in working to improve ground support service standards, as 'you cannot say to passengers that you will be treated one way in the air and another way on the ground'.

Although this message of teamwork and equality may seem like a strong and obvious message, like many of this nature it was not achieved without hard work. Jesudason acknowledges that many of his staff have a high level of formal education, while others have long service and a wealth of experience. So the message that you should 'forget all your education: we are all equal here' needed both repetition and explanation before it was understood and accepted. On the other hand, the style of communication between crew and 'bosses' is now comfortable and easy. During a meeting between Eddie Jesudason and my colleague Daryll Wee, a member of cabin crew walked into the office and gave Jesudason a surprise gift. It was something he had seen and liked on his travels, and she had remembered this and gone out of her way to find and buy it for him. This was in no way an 'apple for teacher' – it was more a token of respect coupled with a refreshing confidence in how to interact with the 'big boss'.

Development, empowerment and learning

Eddie Jesudason deals swiftly and concisely with the concept of empowerment. For him it has, like so many business buzz-words, come to confuse the real issue. 'I've heard it too many times and it has lost its meaning! If I had to define it, I would say that we would give our people the authority to do their job within defined limits and with a high level of consistency.'

For Jesudason, it is the processes leading up to the actual empowerment that are the prime source of interest, and they encompass a variety of elements. First of all staff must be developed, and with customary Singaporean thoroughness SIA have procedures that support development. These include:

- Formal training.
- Exposure to different jobs. SIA find it easy to move people from one department to another to speed up their personal development.
- Working in task forces to address different issues. This allows the task force members to interact with and learn from staff from different divisions.

But for Jesudason, it is what goes on before, during and after the formal processes that is of prime interest. For him, learning is a never-ending process; more importantly, it is integrally linked to making change happen. He is always excited by new ideas, and considers that the most practical leaders must retain this excitement and continually challenge old views in order to see positive results. But this cannot be done alone; once again Jesudason introduces the concept of trust – and elaborates on his own role in making change happen through others.

While the act of trusting others, whether they be individuals, teams or committees, is the key to empowerment for Jesudason, he still retains an active role for himself when it comes to shaping his part of the organization. The active role, however, is in that of activating others to believe in and act in ways that will make the desired changes happen smoothly and effectively. Here Jesudason sees his main role as that of encouraging and convincing his people to move in a certain direction and to believe in the division's goals, but they must not do so blindly or unthinkingly; and it is in helping his people to adopt a challenging yet positive mind set that Jesudason's leadership role becomes closest to that of facilitator. It is also here that he is most often drawn into the role of problem-solver.

For Jesudason, problem-solving is an enjoyable process: interesting, exciting and a challenge. It means having discussions with all involved and adopting a mind set of continually challenging the current process and the *status quo*. Hence, for him, problem-solving is an essential part of his leadership. However, he appreciates that it is often less easy further down the line: others may see rules and regulations in a different light, and here Jesudason acts to help his staff. As far as he is concerned, rules and regulations should be dynamic and not cast in stone, and they should certainly not stifle people's creativity. So Jesudason works with his people; not only with his immediate teams but also by doing everything he can to spread the word that all staff should be confident to challenge rules or processes that they consider to be dysfunctional and to look for creative solutions.

This facilitative approach is especially evident in his dealings with the area of customer service, where the mission is to enable cabin crew to trust their own judgement to a greater extent and to serve the customer in the best way that they can, whatever the circumstances or situation. Given the variety of circumstances that can develop when a plane is in mid-journey and the rules that must of necessity exist, this is a considerable challenge for both Jesudason and his crews.

Planner and strategist

SIA in general works on five-year time horizons when planning, depending on what issues are being addressed. Staffing needs and issues are planned at least five years ahead, so Jesudason does spend quite a lot of his time looking at the medium to long term. However, as he tends to work as much as possible in a team, the horizons are usually dictated by the needs of other team members.

When it comes to formulating a strategy, Jesudason is flexible in approach. He does not have a set series of factors that he takes into consideration, preferring to look at the situation under review and decide what the demands of it are. One thing he does do on an individual basis is to challenge himself about how practical the solutions that are being put forward actually are.

After the strategy has been formulated, Jesudason sees his main role once again as influencer and persuader. The plans and solutions must be explained and sold to all of those likely to be affected, and this is usually done by setting up a series of meetings and discussions.

Of course, the influential strategic leader within a large organization may well be seen as a person of great power, but power is a word that Jesudason does not like. As far as he is concerned, power is only achieved when you have genuinely influenced people, and that influence must travel both upwards and downwards: 'I see power not in the sense of authority, rather I see it as persuasion'. And for Jesudason, if he can pass this view of power down the organization then he will consider himself to have been successful, as he sees his senior cabin crew as not having to use rank to 'control' crew members. Rather, he sees them as learning to go beyond that idea and using their communication skills and the trust that they have learned to develop to motivate their fellow crew members. Once again he emerges as catalyst and facilitator.

Stress? That's not allowed!

The job is busy and involving and makes continual demands. Jesudason, however, believes that he is able to take it all in his stride and, with true Singaporean efficiency, has learned to place work and leisure into different compartments within his life. Life is to be balanced!

The balance within this busy man's life is based upon a combined philosophy of order and goal-setting. Work and leisure are kept in perspective through the process of goal-setting. The goals are kept in mind and used as a focus in whatever he does. This prevents the stress of being uncertain or aimless. It also means that he can be truly focused on whatever activity he is concentrating upon at any one time. It means that he can switch off from work when the day's work is done, and it also means that he can better enjoy his golf and other activities when he is indulging in them: 'sufficient unto the day'.

When he is back at work Jesudason prioritizes everything that he does. He gets involved in a wide range of activities, but, having set his priorities, is able to spend more time tackling those things that are more important or which have longer term impact. This effectiveness is illustrated by his desktop – always clear and without the piles of paper so often seen on executives' desks.

Of course, even with the effective time manager and problem-solver, things do from time to go wrong, and not all initiatives succeed. Here again Jesudason is characteristically philosophical: 'Failure is not the end of the world, it is just one act!'. If failure can be taken as feedback, Jesudason believes that it can be accepted and that you should then move on. Similarly, when things go wrong it should be a case of going back to the drawing board, correcting what you know to have been the fault and then moving on. Jesudason believes that people should make repeated attempts 'to get it right', and only if there is repeated failure or difficulty should there be a major change of direction or reassignment of work.

It is in his approach to organization, to time management and to failure that Jesudason is perhaps most Singaporean in outlook – this 'Spock-like' efficiency is, however, more than counterbalanced by the individual's insistence on trust, on development and on bringing out the creativity in others – a very human approach under the super-efficient exterior.

Summary and conclusions

It is not, however, in the balance between creativity and efficiency that the main messages from Eddie Jesudason lie. Where he really succeeds is in combining a talent for challenging organizational processes with a view to serving the airline's customers as well as possible. For him, change is customer-driven, and as customers' needs change so must the airline. In fact, it must anticipate the changes and keep one step ahead of them. Only then can the service it provides be genuinely excellent.

In an industry where the competition is visibly sharpening and the prospective traveller is continually bombarded with advertisements promising ever better service, greater comfort and methods of looking after you that start before you even leave your front door, the need to stay that one step ahead has never been more urgent. Jesudason is a vital cog in the machine that delivers the service. He can be correctly described as a major service leader, but for him the service is delivered by the team. Most of what he does, whether it is working to inspire trust, facilitating interactions, challenging more junior people to be more creative or setting up team awards for crews, provides evidence of his belief that teams are an essential part of the future of SIA. As an ordered and efficient leader, Jesudason finds the time to work with his teams as much as possible – it is the teams that deliver the service. As he himself says, 'I don't work as an individual; when we win something, we win as a team'.

Key strategic and portable qualities

- Global knowledge of his industry and its context.
- Maintains a customer focus and is passionate about it.
- Keeps his function's core values continually in mind as a guide to action.
- Focuses on the team as the deliverers of both the values and core services that go with them.

- Recognizes the role of leader as a change agent and sees modernization as the goal of change.
- Appreciates that creativity, fun and motivation are all interlinked and must be encouraged.
- Is prepared to win over opponents of innovation through debate and respect.
- Believes the ability of the leader to inspire can come from trust, opinions and the absence of hidden agendas.
- Adopts role of facilitator in helping people rise to challenges.
- Uses goal-setting to control his own stress and to balance the conflicting demands and pressure of work.

Rob Atkins
A strategic approach to total quality

CHAPTER 6

Introduction

Featured on Rob Atkins' business card is an impressive array of qualifications, starting with an MA and moving rapidly on to greater and grander things. However, if quizzed, it would not be these qualifications that he would state are the focus of his pride so much as his lengthy association with Braintree District Council.

For many, especially those who have worked predominantly in the private sector, the very concept of local government brings on a yawn. It is seen as non-commercial, besieged by political agendas, at the mercy of the 'loony left' and basically dealing with matters which, although important, are fundamentally boring. To them, it may consequently be difficult to understand why this particular council has attracted a very dynamic young leader and why he is so passionately proud of his association with it. After all, it's just about collecting litter, processing planning applications and providing meals on wheels to senior citizens – isn't it?

Well, yes it is. But it is also about a great deal more than that, and given the right approach, it is about being extremely businesslike, overcoming difficulties, making radical changes happen and being accepted as a world-wide benchmark for quality. It is the challenge inherent in achieving all of this that has motivated Atkins and kept his name closely associated with the metamorphosis of values, approach and service that is Braintree.

Braintree: the context

Braintree is a very ordinary district in mid-Essex. To many, the name Essex itself has connotations that will provoke a smile, but this piece of Essex is not part of the raunchy east-of-London strip; neither is it far enough north to be able to claim itself as part of rural Cambridgeshire or the Fens. Instead, it sits fair and square in the no-man's land between the prosperous Home Counties and those areas far enough north of London to be able to boast a distinctive regional flavour. It is the sort of place that you see signposted from a motorway, but which you never dream of stopping at unless you have to.

For those who like statistics there are some equally unremarkable figures to help 'size' the District Council. It covers a population of 120 000 and provides a total of 10 800 council houses. Owning other assets to the value of £25 million, it has a turnover of £50 million and employs a total of 1100 people. As a council it is medium-sized; as a business it is quite substantial.

However, as Atkins stresses, for a very ordinary council it has achieved some very extraordinary results. Since 1992, Braintree has won just about every award for Quality in Management that there is going. These include two Government Charter Marks for housing and planning, the Investors in People Award in 1993, the PA/Solace Total Quality Award, ISO 9000/BS 750 for all services (also in 1993), the Arthur Andersen Service Excellence Award in 1994, and the Price Waterhouse World Best Organization Award. One of the awards that gives staff the most pleasure is the one in which it did not achieve first place. In 1993, Braintree was Britain's nomination for the international competition of local authorities organized by the Bertelsmann Foundation in Germany and it came third behind Phoenix in Arizona and Christchurch, New Zealand. It did, however, come in substantially ahead of all UK and other European rivals, and can therefore truthfully boast of being the third-best local authority in the world.

The reception area at Causeway House, the council's main office, has been designed to appear like that of a hotel, and this in turn focuses the staff on thinking 'service' and on treating all callers as customers. Indeed, the welcome that I received at the Braintree reception was more attentive and courteous than you will receive at many a four-star hotel. Just to the right of reception is a display cabinet virtually bursting with the council's myriad awards.

Although demonstrably endowed with awards, Braintree has never been an organization to rest on its laurels, content with what the external world has had to say about it. In 1989 it commissioned a survey from MORI, who compared it with 24 other councils on a number of key criteria for local government. it received the following powerful and satisfying feedback:

Friendliness	1st	Key services	2nd
Efficiency	2nd	Refuse collection	1st
Helpfulness	2nd	Housing	1st
Accessibility	2nd	*Overall satisfaction*	1st
Promptness	2nd		

The end result of all of these awards and accolades has been a high level of interest in Braintree from the media. The council has been accorded the compliment of being named as a benchmark for quality by more than one success on a macro-level from 'commitment to personal service' to '24-hour access to the council's emergency services' or 'consensus amongst the parties'.

It has not always been so good for Braintree. Its one claim to fame is that it was the town in which the textile company Courtaulds was founded, and for 200 years it was by far the town's main employer. Courtaulds employed about 5000 people there in 1984 – the year in which the company closed its Braintree factory, leaving the spectre of large-scale unemployment behind it. It was this fact, rather than any other, that stimulated the council to adopt an initiative called 'Braintree Means Business' in an attempt to attract new employers into the area. It was either that or the near certainty of becoming a total backwater.

Atkins: the formative years

In describing his career history, Atkins is swift to point out the power of the influence of certain strong mentors, and he is certain that his personal development would have been less positive, or at least substantially different, without the benign influence of more than one 'boss' who saw the role of leader as that of coach and mentor.

Atkins joined Wrekin Council in 1979, at the same time as an inspirational CEO, Roger Paine, who was in the vanguard of stimulating change in local government – moving its ethos beyond that of mere administration to that of promoting a belief in customer focus. Atkins worked as a planner for two years and then worked in Paine's unit, ultimately as his personal assistant. During a period of seven years (broken by a period at Nottingham University which resulted in an MBA in planning), Atkins helped tackle a number of problems created by the recession and the necessity for change in local government. The work was creative, involving the creation of grant opportunities and making submissions to the UK government as well as to Brussels.

It was during this period that Atkins cemented his knowledge of local government, but more importantly, he learned the importance of always looking for creative solutions. However, in 1987 he felt the need for a change and looked for a contrast as well. This took him to Arun Council in West Sussex. As an area and as a council, this was completely different from Wrekin. Whereas Wrekin had been free-flowing and adaptive, Arun was governed by systems and procedures and gave him experience of a completely different environment.

Initially, the change was interesting but difficult, and Atkins was struck by the contrast in culture promulgated by his new CEO as well as the impact on culture that can be achieved by one strong leader. Whereas Paine had been creative and entrepreneurial, but disorganized, Atkins' new CEO (John Midgley) was organized, methodical and very procedural in approach. By putting aside any instinctive frustration with this approach, Atkins learned the need for clarity of objectives as well as the requirement for the checks and measures that tell you whether you are getting there.

In speaking to Atkins about these two initial jobs, there is a slight feeling of frustration, of waiting in the wings. As he himself puts it, he had been going through a long period of learning rather than leading. Certainly there had been opportunities to run projects and initiate new developments, such as some trail-blazing market research while at Arun. However, the opportunity to make changes, to move the organization forward, had always been through supporting the CEO and through influencing that person – something in the equation was incomplete, and Atkins had certainly learned, for him, one of the most valuable lessons about leadership, namely that it is difficult for an incoming leader to follow a good CEO. Changes at Arun nudged him into deciding that it was time for a new challenge and time to advance his career. Then came Braintree.

Braintree

In terms of its management culture, Atkins describes Braintree as his spiritual home, but he is swift to point out that as one of the leaders within the Senior Management Team he has been the inheritor of a set of powerful values and initiatives. As an inheritor he has embraced the values as well as the culture to which they have given birth, and has set out to build on, add to and augment the good things which existed on his arrival. Is this leadership? Of course it is! It falls to very few to be the sole and prime initiators of new systems, cultures and approaches. It can be a harder, and equally demanding, leadership job to keep the fires burning and the morale high after the initial impetus is over. It is here, in the longer term, that true character can shine through.

By the time Atkins arrived at Braintree, the Council had already faced the crisis of Courtaulds' closure, which had decimated employment in the area, and had adopted the slogan of 'Braintree means Business' and started to make its mark as a 'customer-focused organization'. Brian Pitman has since stated that strategy is 'focus and hard choices' – Braintree had already realized that and grasped the nettle. Knowing that it had few assets other than the energy and commitment of the people in the organization, it had decided on the strategy of being so good that those looking for an environment in which to grow would not need to look further.

The core values that have driven so many of the processes were formulated in 1984, and are as follows:

1. We are *customer-oriented*
2. We believe in the *abilities of the individual*
3. We must be *responsible and responsive*
4. We believe in *quality*
5. We are *action-oriented*

Atkins came to Braintree because he was attracted by these core values and swiftly adopted them as his own and came to believe passionately in them; they became the drivers of his personal vision within the council, and he considers it an important mission to ensure that they remain as central and relevant in the late nineties as they were in the early eighties.

Before Atkins' arrival there had been approximately five years of changes at Braintree around the themes of the values, but he felt that something was lacking. While the impetus was 'full of sound and fury', he considered that the time had come for the leadership to take a new direction. Not enough attention was being paid to how the changes being introduced were fitting together and being applied consistently throughout the organization. The issue of 'quality' is a good example. You can get excellence in any small part of a large organization by knowing the resources and the best people at it. The key to quality is when you achieve that same level of excellence right through the organization.

A steadying hand

On his arrival, Atkins found an amazing range of activities happening. Initiatives were being taken in a number of different directions, covering the bulk of the council's services. However, although the culture promoted creativity it was not systematic enough to benefit further from it. Atkins set out to introduce systems that would introduce a higher degree of integration, consistency and control across departments. Above all, he set out to ensure that the lessons acquired in one area were transmitted to others. Without integration, the council could not truly call itself a 'learning organization'.

Atkins set out to use the experiences of method and systems that he had acquired at Arun, but whereas these can be considered as primarily management functions, leadership qualities were required of him in introducing management to a creative, fast-moving, yet 'management-averse' organization.

In many respects, Rob Atkins was an ideal person to take on the Assistant Chief Executive role – the informal people-oriented approaches learned at Wrekin blended with the knowledge of structure and management processes acquired at Arun to give the exact skill mix required. His main early contribution was to implement planning procedures across the council and to formulate a quality model as a yardstick for further developments.

It was the fact that Atkins was able to show empathy with the culture of the organization that enabled him to make swift progress with his initiatives – he won people's trust and they then allowed him to make his contribution. After two years of implementing structures that allowed growth and change to happen in a reasonably controlled manner, the controls were in place to allow the safe implementation of a more hands-off approach. The organizing principles were in place, and it was now entirely logical to allow Braintree's culture to carry things forward. To use a fishing analogy: the fish was securely hooked and it was therefore quite safe to let it run, in the knowledge that it could always be reeled in and landed if need be.

Early on, Atkins set his own vision of what the business systems he was implementing should achieve (it was the focus of his MBA dissertation – a comparative study of Arun, Wrekin and Braintree which linked his vision to the established vision for Braintree). Having established broad plans around the corporate vision and its achievement, he set out to give people feedback on how they were progressing towards it. Although he describes his vision as an evolving one, it was capable of concise description. Essentially, it evolved around the introduction of basic business planning methods into Braintree – as Atkins describes it, 'making Braintree really mean Business'. Hitherto, the organization had been functioning principally through its values rather than through the pursuit of a defined strategy, and this was the equivalent of flying an aircraft on the basis that it's a good thing to be airborne, rather than that it's a good thing to be airborne and to know where we're bound and to be able to check the instruments to see whether we're getting there.

The strategist

Rob Atkins describes himself as a strategist by nature and training. With Arun, he had written bulky business strategies and had been frustrated to find that they were neither read or acted on.

In retrospect, he is not at all surprised, and realizes that although a strategy may be full of profound thought and essential detail, it is not an end in itself. Too often, he thinks, people in business are alienated from the aims and direction of the business by the very fact that the strategy is either not communicated to them, or, if it is, it is communicated in a way that does not inspire, empower or illuminate them. In other words, they are baffled, bored or bewildered by it.

As a strategist, Atkins admits that his 'road to Damascus' conversion came when he realized that the strategy document in use at Arun was not serving anybody's needs. For people to act, they need to understand; but to be understood, communication has to meet the needs of the receiver. If the purpose of the strategy document was to communicate and persuade people to follow it, then the strategy statement needed to be simple and digestible. To put it bluntly, you can forgive people for not marking, learning and inwardly digesting a 200-page strategy statement or even for not picking it off the shelves! But nobody can be forgiven for not taking the time to read and assimilate three pages.

The result of Atkins' conversion was a four-page corporate strategy document of the most simple kind. It included the Statement of Purpose (Mission) of the council and the vision on the fourth and final page; it is a concise and hard-hitting document. Nobody reading it could fail to understand where the organization wants to get to and how they can help. Thus the three great drivers of any organization – mission, vision and strategy – are presented in a way that is powerful and accessible. Atkins had put some of the more obscure axioms of leadership into a practical and purposeful framework – an act of leadership in itself!

The strategy document set out the 10 key areas of the council's work, and for each one established a series of objectives and actions to provide guidance for action to council staff, managers, councillors and council customers about the future scope and direction of the council's activities, the values and expectations of the organization and the framework for future policy and operational decisions. The ten key areas are:

Citizenship and democracy
Customer's interests
Quality
Economic and skills development
Environment
Health and community care
Housing
Leisure
Transport
Management (of the council by the council)

Each of the above areas is broken down into four or five components, such as 'Sustain the Council's focus on customer complaints as a key tool for service improvement' or 'Ensure new buildings are safe, aesthetically pleasing and environmentally sound'. For each of the components, Atkins tried to state the message as simply as possible and has tried to adopt as many other ways of working along these lines as possible. 'If a document sounds simple', states Atkins, 'it can empower. People will say Yes, I can do that!'

Atkins' personal philosophy here is born out of that promulgated by Jan Carlson of SAS (Scandinavian Air System, one of the leading quality airlines in the world), with his idea of '1% improvement in 1000 things'. Atkins' approach has been to help people identify 10 areas each in which a 1% improvement could make a noticeable difference. These areas may be as small as ensuring that notices in reception are taken down on the appointed day. 'But if you can get 1000 people thinking like this', he says, 'you will soon generate 10 000 areas of change and improvement. Now you have transformed your organization!'

However, readable documents were by no means all that it took. The process also made other considerable demands on Atkins as a communicator.

The communicator

Like all the other leaders interviewed for this book, Atkins is a great talker, and easily communicates the enthusiasm he feels for his work at Braintree. However, although he has taken on the mission of developing the public face of Braintree in its relations with the media, his main efforts in communicating the strategy have been by a process of diffusion.

Here the tactics have been those of training certain key people in the meaning of the strategy and then encouraging them to filter it down via training and the setting up of working groups. Atkins is keen to point out that in communicating the strategy he does not rely on the issuing of instructions at all. If a strategy is to be adopted successfully in a permissive culture like Braintree's, he states, then you cannot afford to tell people – you must persuade them. Persuasion can mean different things to different people, but to Atkins it is a matter of getting others to look at the targets facing them and, via dialogue and the sharing of information, to show them that the targets are achievable. If you can help them to see how implementation can be achieved and also to recognize that they have a clear role in getting there, then you have the groundwork for successful persuasion.

Is there an iron fist inside the velvet glove? Yes. Atkins makes statements that indicate the level of his determination to implement improvements – going for quality is not optional! However, he does not think that the level of enthusiasm for the quality approach, along with the behaviour changes it implied, would have been nearly so successful if the changes had come as dictates. An example that Atkins likes to quote is the introduction of the council's 'Lookout Scheme'. This scheme, which underpins the council's public complaints scheme, makes the statement that 'everything in Braintree is your responsibility'. Council staff are encouraged to be constantly on the lookout for anything under the council's jurisdiction that is less than excellent – these are complaints waiting to happen. So successful was the launch of this scheme, which emphasized its benefits but also the voluntary nature underpinning it, that there were 450 suggestions for improvement in the first month alone.

So, how much real conflict does he have to handle in getting what he wants? Atkins prefers to talk about challenge. People will challenge the rigour and intellectual integrity of the ideas mooted and also the way it is put forward. If suggestions are made in a naïve or patronizing way then people will point it out, so he does find the need to argue his corner frequently. However, the arguments are almost never about values, as Braintree operates a careful recruitment policy that tries to make sure that those joining subscribe to the overall philosophy.

Common values need not imply cloning, states Atkins. He finds that he is called upon to exercise his persuasive powers frequently, as the passion that Braintree people feel for 'the end product' inevitably generates different ideas and solutions. Being persuasive, for him, means keeping the communication channels open, and he spends considerable time talking to stakeholders: council officers, councillors and trade unions. His strategy is to try to listen, foster the best possible relationships and build up a bank account of goodwill, as he considers that this pays dividends when circumstances get tougher.

Intuition, judgement and politics

As a planner, Atkins tends to look at most problems and most situations from the starting point of logical analysis. If decisions need to be made, he is eager to look at the facts and principles underlying the set of decisions required. So logic is a good point from which to start, although Atkins is swift to point out that the logical principles may not define the final decision. If it is important to eventually have everybody pointing in approximately the same direction, then logic may not play a consistent part in the process of decision-making. It is interesting to note, however, that whereas many leaders swear by their intuition and regard logic and analysis as secondary attributes which may be used to reinforce the intuitive process, Atkins looks at it from the other end of the telescope. Start with the principles – it will reinforce the quality of what you are trying to decide.

One area within organizations where intuition usually serves the leader well is that of organizational politics, and one might consider them to be rife in an institution that, among other things, is controlled by people of different party political persuasions. Surprisingly, in Braintree this is not the case, and having to be politically adept is not something that disturbs Atkins; perhaps he takes it as granted as a necessary skill in local government. The overarching values are strong, and as long as they remain the essential drivers of action in the organization, they will diffuse through all the various political perspectives. A key requirement for all is now to look for successful ways of promoting future success.

Atkins gives an example which is less about politics than about maintaining good communication and being just that little bit inspirational. Before achieving the first Charter Mark Award, the Council had been going through quite a hard time, and people were down. Looking for something to celebrate, Atkins persuaded Braintree to apply for the award, and was delighted when they won it, although the council's management were sworn to secrecy before the public exhibition announcement. On the day of the award they prepared a surprise display in the Town Hall's reception and suddenly wrapped a large banner around the building that read: 'The Best in the World. Now it's time to say, Thank You'.

That day in 1992 they 'over-celebrated' the award, but it worked: the organization was lifted 'six inches higher with pride', and the resultant impetus exceeded Atkins' wildest dreams, as the council then went on to bid for and win every major national management award connected with local government. If the short-term secrecy followed by over-celebration can be termed being political, then, bearing in mind the results, a lot more politics is called for from our business leaders.

Atkins is as dismissive of the concept of his personal power as he is of the use of politics. Once again, for him it is prescribed by the culture of the organization. As far as both he and Braintree are concerned, even if your position carries positional power, there is no call to use it bluntly by issuing orders or seeking to control overtly the activities of others. The key to both power and personal credibility is in being recognized for the contribution you can make and in both recognizing others for what they can do as well as enabling them to do it (a link to facilitation). For him, power is being able to generate a culture in which everybody can be a part of the organization's success – it is a form of power, therefore, that must involve everybody and not be the sole province of just one person.

In effect, Atkins' views about politics and power also impinge upon his views about the future nature of work.

The nature of work

Atkins has read the futuristic books and has taken enough on board to reckon that the future may not just be 'unreasonable' – it may be unimaginable. Consequently, his main aim in thinking about the future is not so much to ponder what it might be so much as to create an organization that is sufficiently flexible to cope with the unimaginable.

How is his own job likely to change? Atkins points to the functions on which he concentrates for effectiveness, those of focusing on charting the future direction, but then helping people by 'opening the doors that will help them achieve'. By this he means that most employees know what it takes to make things happen, but lack the power, connections or confidence to complete the job successfully. Atkins believes that his role will increasingly be one of connection-maker, of coach, of confidence-builder rather than decision-maker. He accepts that the leader will always need to exert some control and will need to have the means of checking that progress is being made in the right direction. However, increasingly he sees his job as that of focusing on those things that make organizations successful and then ensuring that the people in his organization understand them and work with them in mind.

With some pride, Atkins states that there are not many people in the world of local government who actually work with that mind set. For him, the core competencies about which he is talking are founded in the core values of the organization, and the core values have been so clearly and explicitly stated that the line between them and the organization's core competencies has become blurred. This leads to the essential flexibility that has given Braintree, among other things, the best housing and planning services in the UK.

But it is never good enough to make blanket statements about progress; Atkins believes in testing them. In 1993 the council tested the net satisfaction of its Council Tax payers with council services, set against the net level achieved in 1989 (itself a very high benchmark). They found a

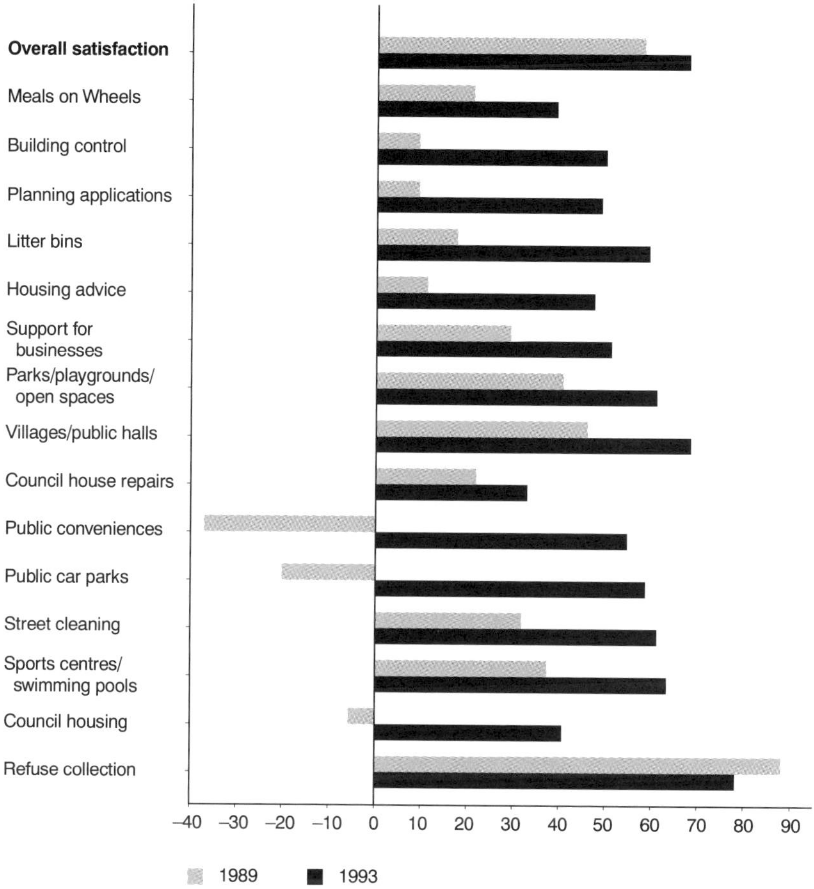

Figure 6.1 Change in net satisfaction with council services 1989–93: Braintree District Council.

significant improvement in satisfaction level in virtually every area tested (Fig. 6.1).

Stretching situations

Although the measurable levels of success have been high, it has not always been personally easy for Atkins. An occasion that genuinely stretched his communicative abilities as well as his views about delegation and support was when he chaired a Second Tier management group whose job was to implement many of the changes in hand. The group members all reported to other directors, and the main challenge facing Atkins was how he would get them to feel like a shadow management team who had real power of action rather than a group who did not have any corporate clout.

Having examined the make-up of the group, Atkins decided with the group that its members needed the experience of chairing meetings, so he stepped aside. The result was to enable members to own their contribution to the Second Tier group. This process continued for approximately 18 months, and the team began to function with much more efficiency and commitment. Then Atkins was given the job of handling a major new initiative, and the group was clearly the right vehicle for the project. However, he considered that the group members were not yet ready to take it forward without his hand being more firmly on the wheel.

This presented Atkins with a dilemma. He had successfully given the group members more control power, but what would happen if he now took it back again? It was now that his earlier investments in the group paid off. At its inception, Atkins had devoted time to formal team-building events, and these had led to higher confidence as well as interdependence. Members were now more easily able to handle the ambivalence of Atkins' position, and after a few hiccups the team was pleased to be in charge of the new project.

Facilitation

So, did Atkins facilitate his way to success with the Second Tier management group, and what are his views in general on the concept?

Atkins accepts that he helped other people to chair the team, and that this may have involved a mixture of instruction, support, advice, and giving feedback, as well as knowing when not to intervene. He prefers, however, to use the word 'support' when it comes to this form of leadership. He is a great believer in enabling others to achieve, and accepts that he may over-delegate. He passionately wants his staff to succeed and accepts that the achievers will want the freedom to do things their way. For instance, he will sign the authorization for them to train in whatever way they think is valuable, whether this be computer skills training or the Open University – facilitation for him is the act of easing the way for others to succeed, and can be done through working alongside people or groups or through enabling them to take further steps on the path of their own development. However it is perceived, he believes that facilitation is 'intrinsic to leadership'.

Stress and failure

The job is a demanding one, but, like many leaders, Atkins has the ability to cope, and so seeks additional demands on his time and energies. He is on the Board of the Strategic Planning Society, is an adviser on management to the Association of District Councils, is a school governor and has various other external functions.

In essence, Atkins has not been good at balancing work and leisure, and reckons that he subliminally designs his life to ensure maximum involvement and pressure. A keen family man, he is worried that his family might suffer from his policy of total commitment.

Like all realists, Atkins will admit to failures. They do not, however, stem from his pressured existence, but are more due to living with the vagaries of local government. One case in point was in connection with Braintree's application to become a unitary council. Atkins chaired the submission, and went out of his way to ensure that it was a 'model submission'. They took it as far as they could, but in the end – after more than a year's work – the decision went against them. At one level Atkins feels that he wasted a year of hard work, but he believes firmly that that sort of response is unhelpful: 'You always have to look beyond the failure to see whether any good can be salvaged from the situation'. He is now active in seeking to design a new working arrangement between the authorities to avoid a retrenchment of positions. He is adamant that response to failure is what makes good leaders better. Being a 'good-time' leader is easy. It is having to pick yourself and others up after a major disappointment that brings out real leadership mettle.

In the case in question, not all the work was wasted, as powerful lessons about procedure and influence were learned and stored for future reference.

Summary and conclusions

Atkins has spent over 10 years at the centre of local government organizations. This has given him the experience of exercising leadership, albeit at a corporate level. In thinking ahead, he wonders whether he may have missed a trick by always being at the centre rather than on the front line, in operational management. He wonders whether a move away from strategic leadership to the leading of service delivery at the sharp end would benefit his personal portfolio. Would a period of 'focusing on the commonplace' in the longer term benefit him as a strategist? These, of course, are questions that Atkins can only answer for himself, and no doubt he will seek out the lessons from his further experiences. In the meantime, his career to date contains meaningful lessons for many other leaders. It falls to very few to set the original vision and to drive the organization to it from start to finish. Many, many more, as in the case of Atkins, have to pick up a vision – perhaps a semi-completed vision – and, through hard work, strategic thinking, flair and above all leadership, help the organization to reach it.

Key strengths and portable qualities

- Insights on clarity of communication.
- Insights on high standards and quality in everything.
- Celebrates organization's successes in a big way.
- Passionately wants his own staff to succeed and may even over-delegate.
- Considers strategy and leadership to be inseparable.

Gill Fenwick
Purpose and mission in South Africa

CHAPTER 7

Introduction

Forget Errol Flynn, move over Kevin Costner; Robin Hood is alive well and living in South Africa. What's more, Robin Hood is a woman!

In September 1995 I had the pleasure of running my first leadership development programme in South Africa. It was a pleasure coupled with some nervousness, as I had been warned that Johannesburg, the location, was the crime and mugging capital of Africa, if not the world. The client was a large multinational company, and I had been told that it was really too early after the demise of apartheid to expect to see any black South Africans among the delegates. That was a pity in one sense, but the friendliness and enthusiasm of the delegates compensated in many respects. My colleague and I were also expecting the arrival of a third consultant who would work with us during the second half of the week, and we were looking forward to working with her with interest.

The course took off right from the start, the delegates displaying a tremendous interest in the subject and enthusiasm for putting the material into action. Only one session proved difficult, and this was the one covering motivation. It developed into an intense debate about whether theories of motivation could apply in South Africa or whether the growth in crime and lawlessness that the country was experiencing rendered them redundant. I forget exactly how the debate was resolved, as in the middle of it one of the participants turned to his colleagues and said, 'Let's see just how far the crime wave is affecting us. If you have had your car stolen or your house burgled in the last 12 months put up your hand'. Each one of the 18 delegates raised his hand'.

The people on the course then turned and laughed when they saw my face – I was dumbstruck. To tell the truth, I was quite depressed about the future of the country until, later that day, I met Gillian Fenwick – the third consultant.

The person

Gill Fenwick is in her mid- to late forties and has a twinkle in her eye that can turn to steel. The steel emerges when she speaks of her mission. It is a straightforward one, delivered as a simple message and backed by a strong vision for the future – things must be changed and they can be changed. The organization that she runs and the methods by which she does so provide the vehicle for the change, and her belief is that if a large number of people contribute in their own small way, then the mountain will gradually be eroded. After all, if you set out to eat an elephant, it is better to slice it up and eat it small slice by small slice. When asked to describe herself, her first response is, 'Well, I'm just a South London schoolgirl who has made good'. There is, in fact, rather more to it than that!

Gill Fenwick is managing director and founder of Percon Development & Training, an organization she started in 1980 as a consultancy for delivering all forms of management, leadership and supervisory training in southern Africa. The consultancy now employs approximately 12 people (consultants and backup staff); in addition, many of the consultants are black South Africans.

For Gill Fenwick, the process of getting to this position has been a long one, but one with a certain logic – almost inevitability – running through it.

Born in London, Gill Fenwick went to Prendergast Grammar School, near Lewisham in south-east London, and from there went on to Teacher Training College (a common fate in the 1960s), where she took a BEd. From there she went on to teach for a year in the north of England. She married, and found herself following her husband out to Zambia – initially to teach, but teaching had begun to bore her, so she left the profession and went to work for the *Times* of Zambia in the Personnel Department. Initially thrown in at the deep end as a Personnel Officer, she was there for five years, and it is some small measure of her energy that, when she left that organization after five years, she was replaced by five people.

During this time Gill Fenwick had married again, to Jim, an accountant, and once again her partner's move had caused her to move, as Jim was offered a position with Anglo American in South Africa. She followed him there, taking a job with a large South African group. The job evolved to that of Internal Consultant, giving advice on personnel matters, but here she encountered two obstacles. The first was the fact that her approach to black development was seen as radical in South Africa in those days. This she could fight against by hard work and determination, but the second obstacle was more difficult to overcome – the glass ceiling. Feeling that she had been overlooked in the promotion stakes because of her sex, she put herself on the job market after four years with the organization.

Nevertheless, she had started to make a name for herself. There were three offers of employment, but Gill Fenwick now had her own agenda: the years in South Africa had given her a keen interest in black African development and a further interest in 'doing her own thing'. One of the approaches made to her was an offer that was hard to refuse – five days' pay for two and a half days' work if she would only give the organization the benefit of her energy and experience by being part staff/part external consultant. This was all the 'push' that she needed: she set up on her own, using her new freedoms to start Percon.

It was as if a growing sense of purpose had finally been liberated, had been shown the green light. Her desire to do something positive for the underprivileged in the oppressive days of apartheid had been growing, and at the same time she had been battling with the realization that a BEd in History was not very useful if you were not teaching history, so she had taken a BA in Psychology and Anthropology, followed later by an honours degree in Clinical Psychology. It was now time to act, to be what she believed in.

Percon: inception, values and mission

Gill Fenwick started Percon as a one-woman show, and set about *delivering the service* through careful analysis of what her clients needed and then *delivering the business*. Her sense of purpose, her desire to do something for the country, was something that was always evident. While the range of programmes eventually offered by the organization covered a wide range of standard topics (including Management, Communication for

Results, Empowering Leadership, Mentoring, Supervision, Team Building and Life Skills), it also added to its agenda workshops and seminars to cover Affirmative Action Initiatives and Corporate Social Responsibility.

From the start, Gill Fenwick set out to make the organization special and sent out the message that it was a South African organization designed to meet South Africa's needs. It can now proudly boast that it enjoys a significant base of major corporates, parastatals and small to medium-sized companies. The company has a developed sense of community responsibility and has been active in black African community capacity-building for a number of years, and has been instrumental in having a major impact on the lives and careers of thousands of corporate and community delegates.

Importantly for Percon, it can also claim to be the delivery agent for the Siyakhula Trust. The main mission of the trust is 'training the nation to build the future'. The word Siyakhula means 'we are growing', and more explicitly the mission is to assist community leaders, CBOs and NGOs to develop skills so that they can effectively initiate and manage developmental and job creation projects to the benefit of their communities. The method is through adapting sound management and leadership principles to meet the varying needs of both urban and rural communities, but approaching them with the same care and dedication as one would work for a major international corporate client.

The Trust that is the formalized vehicle for Percon's community outreach is guided by black South African trustees, all of whom are reputable community leaders. The Trust coordinator is also a black South African. The Trust builds leadership capacity into both the rural areas and the disadvantaged townships and informal settlements. It also works with youth, education and local government. The Trust delivers training all over South Africa and in some of the neighbouring countries.

This is an impressive agenda and set of achievements. But how did it start?

By 1984 Gill Fenwick's efforts had begun to get Percon noticed, both for its inherent professionalism and also for its stated desire to meet South Africa's needs. The mid-1980s were difficult years: it was a repressive, violent period long before anybody had even mentioned the release of Nelson Mandela. It was also a difficult time for foreign companies wishing to do business in the country. In particular, American companies were required to observe the Sullivan Code, which stated that they should either disinvest in South Africa or spend 12% of their payroll on Black Development.

Due to Gill Fenwick's stated interest in black development, she was increasingly asked to pick up this initiative for corporations, and so started to go out into the townships and rural communities to see what could be done with her training and development programmes – how they could be adapted to best serve the communities – a sequence of events that led to the foundation of the Siyakhula Trust.

A crucial decision

Many of the groups with which Gill Fenwick worked were deep in the rural areas, some 600 kilometres out of Johannesburg. Some of the areas were so remote and difficult to get to that, to her amazement, she was often the first white person that the people she visited had seen – certainly the first white woman!

Sometimes she would be greeted with suspicion, but usually the welcome was unconditional: love and acceptance were the norm. On one occasion, the villagers took their welcome to extremes. Unfamiliar with the ways of white people, they had no idea what to feed her. Eventually someone declared that white people only ate pork sausages and chips. With alacrity an envoy was dispatched to Durban and returned with a stockpile. Gill Fenwick was subsequently fed sausage and chips regularly every two hours!

Perhaps it was incidents such as this, or perhaps it was less amusing occasions, such as when Fenwick arrived at a hotel with a black associate only to be told that the associate could not stay at the hotel (her response was to move out with her associate into the black community, where the welcome was better), that led her into a crucial decision. She would not make money from her work in the communities – instead, she would use the work she did with corporations to subsidize the community work.

As her work was now divided 50/50 between the two sources there seemed to be a certain poetic justice in this approach. After four years of successful corporate work she felt that she had the economic freedom to say 'this is what I want to do'.

So we have the picture of a courageous, idealistic person who was prepared to follow the dictates of her conscience. But what of Gill Fenwick, the leader?

Leader and influencer

Looking back to the days when she first started Percon, Fenwick is amazed at how young she was and at the extent of the challenge facing her. Perhaps it was the optimism of youth, or naïvety that prompted her to take the leap into the unknown.

However, in the final analysis, it is more than that. Part of the driving force behind Fenwick's leadership is the fact that she values people. Part of this feeling is innate, while some of it has been learned from those with whom she has worked. She quotes two African concepts as guiding lights in the formation of her vision:

- *Ubuntu* – meaning a feeling of humanity
- *Hlonipha* – meaning respect

and she concentrates on assimilating these principles into her work as a leader and her approach to others.

Over the years Fenwick's vision has grown and expanded. From the initial desire for challenge and autonomy has sprung the driving desire to spread respect for the individual and common sense in the approach to all people, whatever their origins. The method by which she sees these aims being achieved is the development of all the people in South Africa – irrespective of their colour or age.

In spreading the word about Percon, or what it stands for, Fenwick is prepared to influence, to persuade or to inspire. A person with strong public speaking skills, she is quite prepared to use these talents to further her aims. People who have heard her speak as long as 10 years ago have given her the feedback that her message made them think or made them enrol on a development course that has since changed their life. But for Fenwick, the ability to inspire does not simply come from having good communication skills; for her, inspiration comes from within. An inspirational person is excited about life and about what he or she is doing or about what can be achieved. Often this means the ability to convey sincerity, especially about oneself and one's own motives.

But for the leader, states Fenwick, the ability to inspire is related to the creation of the vision – the belief in the future and what is possible – and she is quite prepared to share her vision in words or in print. In communicating to companies she has written:

> One area where the company has a tremendous responsibility towards its staff is in the area of training and development. Time and again we meet employees who talk about how frustrated they are in their jobs. Some companies who prescribe 'affirmative action' would be horrified if they heard their employees commenting that 'in this company you will never get a chance to go anywhere'.
>
> In our work in the community we have discovered many capable leaders who enjoy considerable influence amongst their interest group, whilst at the same time holding down fairly mundane jobs in the corporate field. Since the education system has not delivered, we need to concern ourselves as companies with literacy, adult education and skills training. No company or country will ever be truly successful unless it invests in its human potential.
>
> It is shortsighted to view your staff in isolation from their communities. The socio-economic realities affect their attitudes, self-esteem and mental well-being. Many companies are beginning to accept that the wider community are also stakeholders in their business.
>
> We are continually amazed at what people can do to help themselves. It is a matter of hope and inspiration for this divided and torn country of ours that so many dedicated people are out there working unselfishly to help their communities grow.

Elsewhere, in an article promoting the sponsorship of development projects in the communities by corporations, she writes, 'My challenge to you is to invest in our future by declaring war on poverty and helping all South Africans to help themselves to improve their quality of life'.

In terms of the development work within the communities, Fenwick sees the vision as being achieved by the number of leaders trained by Percon who return to their communities who are able to make things happen and able to sustain the development projects that are so important to the welfare of those communities. While there is also pleasure in seeing her alumni in the corporate sector achieve things and grow, it is progress in the communities that gives her the biggest 'kicks'. In running programmes and helping people, Fenwick recalls that there have been occasions when she has moved from the luxuriously carpeted offices of a major corporation one day to sitting under a tree in a dusty village the next day discussing problem-solving techniques that will help villagers cope better with lion attacks on their cattle.

While quite prepared to launch into the visionary article and to use strong rhetoric, Fenwick is also concerned about the quality of her leadership within Percon. Here she goes out of her way to share the vision and to debate it so that all staff can share the excitement of the challenge of the work that they do. When it comes to her staff, however, far more than rhetoric is required. Given the nature of the work and the stresses of training in even the most favourable conditions, she makes time to support her staff. At first glance this may seem like a more mundane activity, but she is convinced that without a solid basis of support, usually in the form of help with new projects or with discussions about how to tackle a particular problem, the organization will not thrive.

As a trainer, Gill Fenwick appreciates the demoralizing effect of difficult programmes, and so spends a lot of her time talking with her staff and discussing techniques or issues. She sees one of her key functions as ensuring that her staff are successful, and wants them to have good experiences while training, as success breeds success. She has the satisfaction of now being able to add that, with South Africa being at its current interesting state of development, Percon's programmes and processes are really starting to come into their own. In hindsight, she reflects without any undue pride that in 1980 and 1984 her visions were ahead of their time because of the political realities that existed then.

Problems, politics and power

If Fenwick has grounds for satisfaction today, it has by no means always been thus. There have been times when the going has been tough for Percon, economically and politically. In talking about the problems that have beset the organization in pursuit of the vision, she readily quotes Shakespeare:

> When sorrows come, they come not single spies,
> But in battalions

and the battalions require a response.

Usually the response is quick, as Fenwick considers that one of her most useful talents is the ability to think fast on her feet. This fast thinking requires her to analyse the situation and translate the problems involved into manageable components: things that can be dealt with quickly. Fenwick considers that a vital component of her success as a leader is her ability to tackle problems fast and to get them out of the way before they become too serious.

It is when the problems cannot be dealt with quickly that her decisiveness falters and is then replaced by the sheer willpower that gives her such a strong sense of purpose. One such case in point was in the late eighties, when the South African economy was in a serious downturn due to sanctions. Companies were slashing their training budgets and things were looking very serious for Percon. Fenwick and her husband decided to get away from it all at Sun City, a holiday resort some two hours outside Johannesburg. Fenwick was very wound up, as she could not see a way around the problems. Hoping to find peace, she went to a beautiful jacuzzi made in a rock pool. She was the only person there, but instead of relaxing she managed to work herself up into an even greater state of anxiety. Finally, she said out loud, 'I refuse to go under!', got out of the jacuzzi, charged back to her hotel room and told her husband that they had to leave immediately, as she had a lot of work to do. That year witnessed the start of tremendous growth of the business, and Fenwick considers that her blatant refusal to give up or go under helped her tackle the problems and keep afloat.

Some problems arise from office politics, yet Fenwick, being the owner of the company, is seldom drawn into them. Tensions sometimes do exist among her staff, but she tries to keep these to a minimum, primarily through a long induction and training scheme – nobody is pressured into running programmes before they are fully ready to do so, and consequently internal pressures are kept to a minimum. In addition, Fenwick admits to a strong sense of right and wrong. She respects other people's views and would not expect them to be untrue to their beliefs and values. This sets a culture in the organization where honesty and mutual help prevails.

Many of her political dealings have been external to the organization. While she will not succumb to pressure if she feels that something is wrong, she does accept that most people in South Africa have had to come to terms with significant change and that this has not been easy for many – they have had to adapt to things that have challenged their paradigms and basic value systems. Here, her approach is to be patient with these people and not to make them feel guilty. In the days of the struggle, she made sure that Percon was seen to be politically unaligned and she insisted that it said what its staff felt was right and not what was politically correct or expedient. In the long run, this approach has paid off, and so, by ensuring that her politics are essentially value-driven, she has also been politically astute.

When it comes to power, Fenwick states, 'Yes I do have a certain amount of power to get things done and to influence people. I like it that people value my opinions'. However, she adds that she has no interest in going into mainstream politics: she could try to have more power, but chooses not to. Here she acknowledges an interesting paradox in her nature – while she firmly believes that a leader should not allow power to go to his or her head ('It is granted by the people who choose to follow you, it is not a right.'), she admits that if she were to go into politics, she would aim to become a Minister so that she could genuinely get things done and make a difference. Furthermore, her staff consider her to have far more power than she herself admits to! Gill Fenwick admits that it is a paradox, but feels that her ability to laugh at herself keeps her power and many other things in balance.

Views on the future, trust and development

Looking ahead, Fenwick sees change for herself. If she does not change her role in the next five years she fears that she will stagnate, and this has presented her with the challenge of developing her staff to take over from her. The actual future of work, what organizations will actually be like, is hard to predict in South Africa, but whatever does happen, Fenwick wants to be there when it occurs. She predicts that in due course she will probably spend less time in hands-on training or consulting and more time writing or playing a national role in organizing training and development issues. This gives her certain challenges with regard to the development of her people.

Percon's work takes its staff all over the country, and often they have to work in very remote places. It is a core element of the business that Fenwick has to develop and subsequently trust her staff to be where they are supposed to be and to exercise appropriate judgement in various situations. When working in the communities, poor decisions can have serious consequences, so Fenwick has worked hard to ensure that her trust in her staff is displayed in all directions and also that her integrity never varies. This means that if she has said that something will happen she is always at pains to keep her word, and, while she is privy to many confidences, she would not dream of breaking even one – her credibility is at stake.

So the sense of integrity is strong. She can be candid, but on the other hand does not believe that tactless insensitivity makes her any more honest or effective. Offensiveness is no substitute for tactfulness, and integrity can still be displayed tactfully. Fenwick quotes the concept of *Utumtn* which means that 'a man is only a person through other people'. It is a concept that transcends both empathy and integrity.

When it comes to developing her people, Fenwick states that she is fortunate to have 'fantastic people' working for her. They are keen to do their best and aim to be very responsible. Of course there are weaknesses, but they are mainly related to differing levels of experience and exposure. This means that Fenwick will work with each staff member individually as coach and mentor; fortunately the organization is still of a size that permits this. As part of the learning process mistakes will inevitably happen, and Fenwick is prepared for this.

When a mistake occurs she devotes time to talking the individual through the process so that the person understands why the decision was wrong. Nevertheless, Fenwick confesses that her standards are high, and while anybody can make one mistake once, repetitions are not welcomed!

As part of her mentoring role, Gill Fenwick tries to make herself available if staff want to discuss a problem or put forward a new technique or project. It is important to her that her staff have positive experiences at work, and if having exposure to her time and expertise helps then they are entitled to it. As she is frequently out of the office this means that she spends a lot of time talking on the phone after office hours. Having devoted many hours to her staff's learning and development, Gill Fenwick is quite prepared to add the 'tough manager' role to her approach – if her staff want to learn something or start a new project, then she expects them to be committed and to follow through.

Gill Fenwick believes in empowerment, as illustrated above. Indeed, she adds with a smile, that as she wrote Percon's programme entitled 'Empowering Leadership', it would be hypocritical for her not to put it into practice. One example of how she managed to put empowerment into action was when she herself was sinking under a huge workload and realized that this was making her a 'work blockage' within the organization. In order to confront the problem she discussed it with her trainers, and it was decided that they would assume responsibility for dealing with communities, evaluating requests for the Siyakhula Trust, and preparing proposals for funding. As part of the transfer, Gill Fenwick showed her staff how to do the costings and how to write the proposals while they themselves designed an evaluation document and took on the work of informing the communities of the work of the Trust.

To quote Fenwick: 'This is a significant part of the business and I am thrilled at the way that they have taken up the challenge and run with it. They justifiably feel more ownership of the situation and know that I will back their decisions in this area'.

Fenwick also states: 'Learning in the work place? Well if you stop learning you might as well give up!'.

Teams and facilitation

Percon is small enough to work as a team, and Gill Fenwick encourages this. However, owing to the nature of the work, there are in fact several teams within the organization, and Fenwick encourages the team approach even though the trainers are often dispersed all over the country. It is hard to get everybody together for monthly review meetings and Fenwick recognizes this, but she states that this makes it even more important for everybody to consider themselves part of the larger team.

So, how is this done? It is all a question of atmosphere and responsibility. Fenwick has worked hard to promote a spirit within Percon where everybody tries to help each other and nobody can get away with saying 'that's not my job'. Consequently, both hard and soft approaches are at work. The message is soft, but the enforcement of it can be tough, and Gill Fenwick is prepared to be tough in getting what she considers to be the right approach prevalent within the organization as she passionately believes that the future lies in the benefits that empowered work teams can bring to most situations.

As the boss, Fenwick has a number of tools at her disposal for making the right sort of teamwork happen. Sometimes the best approach is via team and social events, such as those built around the organization's cricket team. On a more pragmatic note, however, she sees her function as that of smoothing the process – of facilitating the interactions of people within her teams as well as helping the different teams to communicate and work with each other better. For her, the concept of facilitation means 'to make easy', and as a trainer that is something that she tends to do most of the time. It is for her, however, a concept that can also be readily applied to leadership situations, and is one of the keys to her effectiveness as a leader. Although she certainly does not believe in doing the job for people, she does consider that the leader should help people to share experiences, encourage dialogue between groups, give feedback on progress and mentor those who are experiencing difficulties. There are also many occasions when the leader is the best placed person to help others make connections, both mental and physical. Moreover, as the organization grows in size and complexity, more of her time is spent on these facilitative leadership processes.

Thinker and strategist

Gill Fenwick sums herself up as a dominant idealist, and these personality traits affect her approach to rules, to meetings and to the formulation of the organization's strategy, with the knock-on effect on its culture.

As the originator of many of the rules and regulations within Percon, she is of the opinion that adherence to rules and procedures frequently sets the individual free rather than constrains. However, they are not there to be followed blindly, and she recognizes the need to question and re-examine them from time to time and for the leader to encourage the team to do this. She also sees the need for all to change and be flexible when the time is right. As a dominant personality, she knows that she is likely to have a major impact on meetings that discuss policy. She is prepared to listen to alternative views, especially if what is being said makes sense, and she will then support the group decision, but if she considers that what is being proposed is wrong, dangerous or unethical she will hold her ground.

It is this fighting streak that has been so important both to the growth of Percon and to the personal growth of Gill Fenwick; it is perhaps also the cause of some of the dilemmas with which she battles. Here is a person who appreciates creativity in others and sees the need for rules to be challenged from time to time, yet here also is a person who recognizes her dominant nature and often struggles to let go. As the original entrepreneur she can see the extent to which Percon's culture is influenced by her original vision, her values and her personality. She accepts responsibility for what the organization is today, yet is proud to comment that her staff are now making their unique contributions to both culture and policy. In looking at Fenwick and Percon, it is interesting to observe the conflict between the need to dominate and the feelings of guilt at having dominated. In addition, it is interesting to see how hard Fenwick can be on herself – when she gave her staff the first draft of this chapter, they specifically wanted to comment that she had underestimated the beneficial impact on the organization's culture of her energy, empathy and sense of humour; all things that made it good to work at Percon.

As the original entrepreneur, Fenwick still devotes considerable time to formulating the organization's strategy. As the leader, she is certainly also the key strategist. Her main period for strategic thinking is the South African summer, which is at its peak in December and January. Before this she will have spent many hours gathering information, reading widely and observing trends. If what she sees during the year warrants specific strategic thinking that will result in decisions or a change in direction, then she will make the time for the decision-making. However, normally it is the high summer that will see her analysing the trends and formulating the strategies accordingly.

Like most busy people, Fenwick has to fight for the time to invest in quality thinking. Public holidays are a good time for this, as she can go into the office, where information is available but all is quiet. When she is working on strategies she likes to write down facts and potential plans until she sees a pattern starting to emerge. From this pattern will come various potential courses of action, which must then be evaluated. Fenwick feels the need to ask herself 'what if?' questions, and from this analysis will come an idea of the potential consequences.

Once again, Fenwick has to battle with the implications of having founded the organization. As the person with the original vision, it is all too easy to be the sole strategist – to overcome this risk, she involves her team in a SWOT analysis to examine where the organization currently stands and to get staff members to contribute to strategy formation. Then it is a question of holding back; not dominating proceedings, but acting as a facilitator where necessary.

The battle with stress

Like many people who lead busy lives and who are driven by their ideals, stress, or rather the effects of stress, is a factor to be reckoned with.

Gill Fenwick has a theory about stress – if you have one source of stress it will defeat you, but if you have several you take them in your stride. For her, the main enemy is migraine and tension headaches. She suffers from so many of them that she now just carries on regardless, and has learned to hide the fact that she has them from others. When she is actively training other people she takes pride in the fact that nobody would guess that she had a pounding headache, and states that if you have a leadership position within a business you are not going to escape pressure, and that if you can relieve it, do so, but if you cannot, 'just put your head down and get on with it!'.

Relieving the pressure is done in a variety of ways. Fenwick enjoys reading, bird-watching and spending time in her garden. Other sources of relaxation include tending her Persian cats or working on huge jigsaw puzzles, a different form of problem-solving which she finds very relaxing. She also finds it enormously helpful that Jim, her husband, supports her 100% in her business endeavours, something that helps greatly when things are busy or difficult. Fenwick also finds a sense of humour useful: 'every leader should have one – it helps if you can see the funny side of a situation and laugh at yourself; this stops you taking yourself too seriously and getting things out of perspective'. One situation that she looks on with wry humour concerns the amount of time that she and Jim are able to spend together. When she was very busy in the early years, taking two additional degrees through correspondence, she encouraged her husband to spend time with his friends and pursue his own interests. Now that she is not as busy on a constant basis she would like to spend Saturday and Sunday with him, but he is the one who has commitments now. Consequently, she often goes into the office and works until he estimates that he will be free.

Summary and conclusions

In Gill Fenwick we have a portrait of the old-fashioned idealistic leader in a very modern setting. Driven by her mission to change the face of South Africa, she has incorporated this mission into the vision for Percon. Education and development are the key, and the growing influence of Percon, with its ability to subsidize work in one sector by the profits from the other, makes turning the key possible. Perhaps the comparison with Robin Hood is unjust, as Robin Hood reputedly stole in order to subsidize the poor. Nevertheless, both leaders are (or were) driven by a strong sense of natural justice, and courage plays a part in both lives.

Did Robin Hood work too hard, and did he battle with his ability to let go? Neither legend nor history has favoured us with that knowledge.

For Gill Fenwick, who sees herself able to do something positive in a very dynamic but changeable situation, the dilemma of how much to keep a hands-on approach and how much to let go is a real one. However, as a change agent she recognizes the need to move on and to avoid personal stagnation, while at the same time not sacrificing any of her ideals. The energy, idealism, commitment and tenacity remain as strong as ever – it is probably a question of 'watch this space!'.

Key strengths and portable qualities.

- Has a clear mission that gives purpose to all other activities.
- Has energy that is applied and directed towards specific goals.
- Identifies mores and values which govern the approach of doing business.
- Recognizes the power of both the spoken and written word in inspiring others and changing mind sets.
- Reserves time to support subordinates.
- Fights to find time for quality thinking and strategic planning.
- Developer of own staff and facilitator of process.

David Richardson
Walking the tightrope in the music world

CHAPTER
8

Introduction: why should the conductor get all the glory?

Recently, interest has been shown in the concept of the orchestral conductor as leader. Time Warner have produced a compulsive video featuring the styles and approaches of a number of world-famous conductors (most of them dead!), and in it have drawn the metaphor of the conductor as inspirational leader, as the focus of the team, as coordinator of complex activities and as leader from the front. The video also conceded that the majority of the conductors were strong characters, often wilful and, above all, showmen.

So what of the people who have to lead the orchestra leaders, who have to work with the showman conductors and also balance the competing demands of the musicians, other executive sponsors and the general public? What of the CEOs – the people who are ultimately responsible for placing the product before the public?

It was this question that led me to speak to David Richardson, who is Director of the Eastern Orchestral Board (EOB), based in central London. As someone who cannot tell a crotchet from a quaver, and whose knowledge of jazz, although in itself limited, greatly outstrips my knowledge of classical music, I confess to feeling some relief that I would not be speaking to a conductor and consequently that I would not be called on to demonstrate knowledge of things musical.

London has many oases of peace amid the traffic, the tourists and the bustle of everyday life. Stratford Place, the home of the Eastern Orchestral

Board, is one of these oases, a cul-de-sac made up of impressive Georgian properties with grand facades and imposing front doors. The EOB, however, is situated in garret-like offices on the top floor of one of these buildings, and on a hot summer's day the visitor will arrive there hot and breathless.

The person

As Director of the EOB, Richardson describes himself as both a musician and a manager, although it is not now as a musician that he is employed. Aged about 50, he is tall, of slim build and has the aesthetic air of an artist about him. If he were to be placed in a police line-up with the intent of finding the musician among executives from a number of different walks of life, the job would not be too difficult – Richardson would not escape.

Richardson has been the CEO of four of the major orchestras in the UK and the USA over a period of 23 years. These have been:

- The Hallé Orchestra
- The Scottish National Orchestra
- St Paul Chamber Orchestra, Minnesota
- Bournemouth Symphony Orchestra and Bournemouth Sinfonietta

He now has the responsibility for leading an organization whose job is to encourage the spread of musical arts over a large part of England. The demands of this career have left Richardson with a wealth of thoughts about leadership, influence, politics and power.

Like many people in executive positions within the music business, Richardson's training was as a musician. He took degrees in music at Manchester University and The Royal Manchester College of Music, specializing in the trumpet, the piano and singing. His ambition was to be a professional musician, and his eventual specialization led him into starting his career as a professional trumpet player.

After a short period of time, events and exposure to other musicians drew him to the conclusion that, although he was competent, he would never be the star. There would be work as second trumpet but not as the principal, so, having faced up to the unwelcome truth that has to be faced by the overwhelming majority of talented people, namely that there is always someone out there who is quicker on the draw than you, he decided to go for a job that would keep him busier and exercise other talents. He applied to BBC Radio as a music producer.

Looking back, Richardson considers himself lucky to have got in to the BBC and that it gave him a firm grounding in the music business. He spent four years in production. Here he picked up experience, but it was at this time that the hidden entrepreneur in him made itself known, and he began to feel frustrated by the bureaucracy of the BBC as a large organization.

During his time at the BBC, Richardson had worked closely with his boss, Gerald McDonald, who had also become his mentor, so when McDonald left the BBC and joined the New Philharmonic Orchestra in London, it only took one invitation to persuade Richardson to join him and start him on a career of orchestra management that has been part of a distinguished career in the arts. Throughout this career, however, Richardson has thought of himself as a musician who is a manager rather than the other way round – a trait that he considers common among people in his profession.

Like most leaders, Richardson would describe himself as a survivor, and he also insists that the lessons he has learned about leadership have been a product of his entire career, rather than the experiences of his current post. Consequently, the context in which David Richardson's leadership is examined is not only that of the EOB but also of the major orchestras that he has led and influenced.

The context

The orchestras that Richardson has managed are similar to most commercial organizations in so far as they have a core of 'sharp end' customer-facing specialists and, to back them, a whole range of support staff and administrators. What makes them different from most other organizations is that the organization becomes the product when it is in production, and consequently exists on two different planes which overlap and are interdependent. This fact gives the CEO the difficult job of both managing the support side and balancing these efforts with taking care of the artistic side, which, as orchestras resemble businesses far more than they used to, involves finance, the law and fund-gathering. When Richardson first became involved with orchestras, he was more involved in the artistic management of the orchestra than he was to be later. However, with the passing of the years and the growing sophistication of the organizations, his artistic involvement has shrunk. Despite this shrinkage, the challenge of having to lead, influence and negotiate with conductors, musicians and others on the artistic side was always with him.

The EOB is different. Having grown out of the Eastern Authorities Orchestral Association, which was founded in 1965, it is a unique and successful partnership of local authorities and sets out to fund professional orchestra concerts in 11 eastern counties comprising 20% of the land mass of England.

Making use of its two main sources of income – subscriptions from 65 member authorities and two regional arts boards – it supports approximately 180 concerts and 30 educational projects each year. The EOB sets out to do far more than just support: it encourages the 'adventurous programming and performance of music by contemporary composers', and its innovative education programme encourages multicultural work as well as projects in schools. In essence, the Board wishes to enhance the arts and education strategies in the region, its staff acting in an advisory capacity and making sure that what it does dovetails with existing musical provisions.

The EOB summarizes its aims as:

- To raise the awareness, understanding and appreciation of music, and especially orchestral music.
- To encourage participation in music throughout the community.
- To increase the audience for live orchestral music
- To encourage local authority departments to collaborate, enabling educational events to be linked to orchestral concerts.

In all, this places Richardson into the role of leading an organization and leading a wide variety of initiatives connected with theatre organization but over which the Board has no authority. The role calls for the talents of influence, administrative flair and diplomacy – all of which were called for and exercised in his previous positions.

The board usually includes prominent people in the community who can use their connections to the orchestra's financial and political benefit. The Americans coined a pithy job description for arts and charity board members: 'to give, get or get off'. These people may also have other reasons for their involvement, including the social status that being on the board of an orchestra brings and the opportunity to mix with international conductors. The CEO must accurately gauge the motivations of the various members of his Board in deciding how best to present the strategy.

The demands of the role

The job of being leader and general manager of an orchestra places a number of competing demands upon the job-holder.

The first and probably most important demand is to take on the role of strategic leader and to ensure that the organization continually looks to the future. This can be difficult in an organization which can focus too intently upon its product and not show too much concern beyond the immediate 'delivery' of that product. So the leader has to ensure that the orchestra not only has an artistic strategy that is dynamic and sufficiently catholic in approach to support all views, but that it also has a business strategy that can be promoted in a way that augments the artistic side. To do this it is necessary to work with the conductor, who as the musical director will be seen much more as the leader by the public.

One of the main changes, therefore, is to ensure that the organization emerges with one single set of coordinated aims, which will have the result of making the CEO and the musical director speak with one voice on matters of policy. So in the end the job, while having a strong strategic element, comes down to that of having to manage relationships.

The relationship management in no way stops with the conductor. The orchestra always has a Board and a Chairperson, while the Board members act in the capacity of non-executive directors who not only have an advisory function but can also bring community interests and considerable pressure into play in order to make their views heard and put into action.

When it was put to Richardson that he must often have felt like the 'pig in the middle' he put a more positive slant on it. When thought of dispassionately, the situation represents a triangle. At the apex are the Chairperson and the Board, at one corner is the Musical Director, who undoubtedly holds a number of musical agendas, while on the third corner sits the Director, with the complex task of balancing the triangle. In other words, the possibly competing influences of the Board and the Musical Director must not be allowed to overshadow or compromise each other, while neither may be allowed to divert the orchestra from what the Director perceives to be a sensible business strategy.

In recognizing the viewpoints of the various interested parties, the CEO also has the job of ensuring that the orchestra presents a logical and united face to those other key stakeholders: the founders, the general public and the orchestral players (as both employees and product).

So, among the various executive responsibilities the CEO has a major PR role to perform, and the effectiveness of this role will depend upon his or her ability to ensure that conflict between the interested parties is minimized and contained. In looking at this aspect of the CEO's role, Richardson is less keen on the description of the function as peacekeeper – you sometimes have to allow a certain level of conflict – than he is of the term facilitator. There will always be a number of dynamic and potentially explosive interactions taking place. The main characters in these interactions are the administrator of the musical side of the orchestra, the Board and others in the form of the various stakeholders. All of these parties may have different objectives, and somehow the CEO must ensure that they communicate and interact in such a way that the orchestra, as opposed to any particular party, benefits.

In so far as the CEO does not have direct authority over all of the parties (despite being the acknowledged leader), the job of facilitating the interactions is made more complex. While running orchestras, Richardson has noticed the increasing complexity of the work and the fact that he was having to spend more time running the organization through means other than straightforward direction. Being able to exert influence became more and more important, as also was the way in which influence itself was exerted. Did one take people aside individually and try to persuade them of the correctness of a certain viewpoint or were different skills needed when dealing with the various groups, all of which might have competing objectives? Of one thing Richardson was sure. When he had tried methods of leadership that did not rely solely on a directive command and control approach, the results were more positive and longer lasting.

Vision, inspiration and succession

When asked whether he has thought up and pursued his own vision during his career, Richardson is cautious in his response: 'Well, yes and no'.

When he took on his first major orchestra management job at the Scottish National Orchestra (SNO) at the tender age of 31, he confesses that he did not have a personal vision for it and that he felt no burning need for one. He had joined a stable, well-run organization that was doing well and succeeding in its projects. This very fact enabled him to watch what was going on and to learn from the organization itself.

The nature of this learning was vital both to Richardson and, in time, for the SNO itself. Richardson learned by managing the existing processes and by watching carefully what was and what was not possible. Once he had learned these essential lessons he was able to refine and develop the 'possible' along lines that he himself had conceived. During his eight years in Scotland he made a number of changes with a view to what the SNO could become. These included:

- Persuading it to extend its range of performed work.
- Inaugurating new foreign tours.
- Developing recording as a mainstream activity.
- Pushing up sponsorship from contributing nothing to approximately 10% of revenue.

Richardson concludes from the success of his approach with the SNO that the vision need not come from within the leader him or herself. He considers that it is equally valid for the leader to fit into the prevailing circumstances and react to them over time, seizing the opportunities that he or she finds. This does not fit in with prevailing theories about the leader as change agent, but that does not worry him.

An example of his reactive approach is given by Richardson. When the Scottish Opera (until then a part-time company, for which the SNO had played for two short seasons) became a full-time company and increased its orchestral requirements, this caused a separation and posed a major threat to the SNO, which had to fill its former opera periods with new work.

When this happened, Richardson sat down for a major brainstorming session with himself. His vision was that the SNO would continue to flourish and have just as high a profile as if the breakaway had not taken place. So how was this situation to come about?

The 'reactive vision' was that of placing a new emphasis on marketing. Richardson brought about the change via a series of initiatives that included bringing in a consultant from Chicago to introduce American methods of subscription marketing, telephone sales and client mail, new sponsorship initiatives and starting up seasons of 'proms' in three new sites. The result was that the orchestra, as opposed to suffering, tripled its subscriptions in three years.

While the marketing initiative was largely Richardson's brainchild, he worked hard to ensure that it found favour with other stakeholders, taking time to bounce ideas off them; in particular, he involved Alex Gibson, the Musical Director. Thus, while accepting that he found it easier to do the initial work in translating the vision into plans and activities himself, Richardson remained aware that concepts conceived totally in isolation would suffer at the implementation stage.

A time for inspiration

Although often preferring the role of planner or that of influencer, Richardson concedes that there are times when the leader has to take a more up-front inspirational role. One particular case in point was at the Bournemouth Symphony Orchestra and Bournemouth Sinfonietta whom he found to be in bad shape when he joined.

The whole organization had become affected by weak management and the effect of a recent attempt to make musicians redundant, which had then been withdrawn under pressure. Morale was low, and there was a great deal of bad feeling between individuals. On top of all this, the Sinfonietta had for many years depended on its relationship with Glyndebourne, the world-famous opera venue in Sussex, for a major part of its revenue stream, and when Glyndebourne announced that it was going to form its own orchestra this represented nine weeks' loss of work. But it was more than just the work loss: the change stirred up a great deal of fear and morale sank lower.

Purposeful action was needed, and Richardson did two things. First of all, he set out on the route trodden by so many leaders in the past. He talked to people, listened to their fears, spoke to them about the good things that the orchestra still represented and talked about the work that was still in place. Then he backed up his words with action.

The action came in the form of a strategy to restore financing reliability and give it new artistic purpose. In order to ensure that the strategy was both refined and acted on, Richardson appointed an education officer to look at the detail of the ways in which the problems of obtaining new markets and growing revenue streams could be addressed. While Richardson's time was still caught up in balancing the triangle of influence and making sure that the organization's image was improved, he made special efforts to inspire the Education Officer to come up with ideas, and supported him when he did so. Eventually, he was able to prove both to the orchestra and to the public that a firm and workable strategy was in place and that it would sort out the problems.

Another occasion when Richardson felt the need to throw energy and inspiration at a situation was on taking over at the Hallé Orchestra. Here he found a set of circumstances that must be feared by many an incoming leader – the ghosts of the past.

The Hallé – perhaps Britain's most well-known and best-loved orchestra – had been under the same CEO for 32 years. This had been a period of sound financial management, but artistically it had failed to move on to the same extent as other major orchestras. Its great period had ended with the death of the charismatic Sir John Barbirolli in 1970. Richardson detected a strong need for change. The organization was living in the past and was taking its supremacy for granted. What was now needed was a new relationship with the City of Manchester, in which its views were more actively taken into account. There was also a paramount need to move on to explore new ground musically.

In order to make the changes he had in mind possible, Richardson set out to challenge the *status quo*. He asked people to consider what was possible and whether it would work, and tried every means of jolting them out of the traditional ways of thinking. It was a difficult job, as persuading people to move from the tried and tested, especially when, superficially, it still seems to be working, is difficult. Richardson's view was that it was necessary, and he put his energies into trying to convince those involved that more of the same would only lead to decline, whereas a change of direction should lead to a new golden age. In order to help him he brought in a new Musical Director with similar forward looking views, and together they set out to ring the changes.

Politics and power

In the end, Richardson was not as successful in implementing his strategy for change in the Hallé as he would have wished. He does not put this down to any flaws in the strategy or even to his ability to communicate it and to inspire others while doing so; after all, he had succeeded before. The problem came through the political realities of the situation.

Richardson is sanguine about the politics of working in an orchestra. The very nature of the organization, with the separation of the Board, the musical arm and the staff, makes it, in his opinion more political than many others. Add to this the average size (130 people) and the expected turnover (£5 million), and all the ingredients for infighting and intrigue are present, with the CEO in the uneasy position of fulcrum.

If he has a dislike, Richardson considers it to be in dealing with political situations. He has a natural aversion to manipulation and to circumstances that have strong undercurrents of emotion, hostility or intrigue. In addition, he does not consider himself to be good at spotting the hidden agenda. Looking back at the Hallé, he does not think that he did that well there, and wishes that straightforward approaches could have been more acceptable. Perhaps it is the strong streak of personal integrity that makes many a leader so good (and which the author believes is an essential prerequisite for emergent leaders) that can also leave them vulnerable, and perhaps many of them plan to fail by not planning how to deal with the various political contingencies.

In the end, the last word goes to Richardson: 'Very often there comes a point when you seem bound to lose whatever you do. To avoid it you must learn to watch your back, read the signals, heed the warnings'.

Power and politics are often spoken of in the same breath, and if Richardson does not invest much time in thinking about organizational politics, by the same token he does not think of his role in terms of power. When pressed, he thinks of this job as leader in terms of the authority he has earned, the influence that he is able to exert and the imagination that is required of him to be effective and which he has a duty to bestow on the organization. If Richardson has a passion, it is in ensuring that his imagination and personal creativity get an airing via the sort of power that he wants to wield, but he stresses that he is not interested in power as a commodity for its own sake.

It is with the EOB that Richardson currently finds the most opportunity to exercise power via creativity.

Although it exists to promote orchestral concerts, as an organization the EOB does not seem to fit with the Arts Council's model of an arts organization, as it was created as an attempt to enable orchestral developments to happen where previously they did not take place. As its CEO, Richardson sees his and the organization's job as being that of a broker, as its task was that of creating a greater volume of activity without creating additional orchestras. As a broker leader, he has the scope to make new things happen by being both personally creative and influential, and for him this is where the greatest satisfaction lies – it's the main turn-on.

It is often said that power is the 'big turn-on', and Richardson confesses that he is intensely interested in promoting the EOB as a leader within its own industry. This can be done by spreading good practice and developing a demand for concerts where previously there was none. If this is power, he states, then this is the sort of power that interests him. As an outsider, it is difficult to think of any effective leader who does not hold a strong interest in promoting his or her own organization or department. Preoccupation with one's own personal power may pre-empt personal downfall, but dedication to promoting the power and standing of the organization must be part of the bedrock of effective leadership.

In talking about the organization as leader, Richardson has additional views on the power of the team within it. The leader of the organization must try to create a team with the same values and objectives, as it is this team that will create the energy to make additional creativity happen. All too often the leader fails to recognize the benefits of being backed by a solid synergistic team, whereas the leader must always recognize its contribution. Only with this recognition and feedback in place can the concept of the organization as leader genuinely become reality.

So what is Richardson's approach to working with his teams?

He is a great believer in the facilitative approach to teamworking, and his definition of this approach is that the leader must help team members to achieve those things that they want to achieve. To do this it is necessary to help them decide on those objectives and then to work with team members to help them achieve them. For example, in his current role with the EOB the objective of both his team and the people with whom the organization works is to run more and better concerts. Richardson's job is to work with those teams in order to help him address the obstacles and to generate new ideas. Just issuing orders will not liberate the creativity or ownership of decisions required. Increasingly, Richardson feels that the nature of his work as a leader is moving in this direction, and he believes it to be on the increase, based on his observations of other leaders in the music business.

The future

When asked to look ahead to both potential changes in the way that he works and potential changes in the music world, Richardson's views tally with commonly held beliefs about changes in the greater world of commerce and employment.

He foresees a future where the nature of government support of the arts will change. Although the National Lottery is already making a difference to capital schemes, and will increasingly, he believes, provide a source of operating revenue, he considers that there are already too many orchestras and 'arts organizations' in existence, so that additional funding from the lottery, over and above that given by the Arts Council, will not permanently counteract the large fixed costs of symphony orchestras. This means that the future will mean more casual employment and fewer orchestras, giving proportionately fewer opportunities for musicians, and with the resultant necessity of greater flexibility of attitude and employment from everybody in that industry. How like the outside world!

Richardson is not, however, adverse to change. In fact, he likes it.

Although he is not in favour of change for its own sake, he has a positive attitude that regards change as a benign challenge. 'It is impossible to say that this year's values will still be acceptable in five years' time, and so you have to look at changing times as something of interest. Within a brisk rate of change it is not possible to look to see how your organization can itself change for the better', he states. He also considers that the rate of change challenges the individual to adapt, to learn and to be more flexible. Citing a mundane example, he says that most executives now type their own letters. Is this a disadvantage? Certainly not! It brings you closer to the work and promotes a far greater sense of ownership than was felt in the past. Richardson considers it vital that the leader should encourage an open, indeed opportunistic, attitude towards change among others. If this can be achieved, then the effects of the dilemmas and uncertainties of changing business scenarios can be minimized, and those involved will be much better able to tackle them themselves.

The generation of trust

As someone who is wary of organizational politics, I was interested in Richardson's views on trust and its effect in motivating the organization.

One of the greater challenges in his career came early on in his time with the Bournemouth Symphony Orchestra. Richardson arrived to find a conflict between the orchestra's management and the Friends of the Bournemouth Orchestra, which have been acting to support the players in fighting against change and were critical of everything that the management did.

Richardson realized that it was critical to win approval for the new strategy for the orchestra, both from within the orchestra and from those outside. Consequently, he embarked on a crusade that lasted several years to overcome the problem. Although he was personally confident in the strategy, it took a lot of his time and patience speaking to people, answering their concerns and, in effect, fighting the same battle over and over again.

What the battle meant in terms of actual activity was that Richardson had first to line up his arguments and then to test their validity through a number of statements, made both publicly and privately. The statements were delivered through a series of after-dinner talks, statements to the press and exhortations at meetings. This dealt with the public battle to win the community's trust in the strategy, but there were further battles to be fought. A number of individuals, both inside and outside the orchestra, were sceptical about the strategy, and he needed to win their trust. On many occasions this meant that Richardson had to visit people in their homes outside working hours for long, intense conversations in which the issues were debated and the essential trust gradually won.

In retrospect, Richardson feels that for months he scarcely ever seemed to be off duty. As a result, he considers that trust can be won, but that it takes work and investment of time and effort. It is not easily given, but once won it is something that both parties must fight to keep.

Much the same sequence happened when he joined the Hallé. The circumstances of needing to introduce changes after a long period of stability demanded a lot of him, and he is of the opinion that each new leadership opportunity makes major demands on the incoming leader in this respect. 'It is something you have to repeat again and again if you want to develop a career as a leader.'

Over the years he has developed special approaches for dealing with musicians, who represent the bulk of his 'Staff'. 'They are very self-contained people', he says. They want to be involved in the undertaking, but as a rule dislike making hard decisions, and shy away from them. So if you want to win their trust, if you want to persuade them that involvement – power – also brings responsibility, you must adopt a slow and careful approach. In this way they will be drawn into the process of decision-making and will eventually accept the necessity of some hard decisions.

Strategic thinking – an absolute necessity

If there are members of one profession that Richardson envies, it is those who inhabit the world of academia. Not that Richardson himself has pretensions in this direction or that he considers himself to be overtly academic. He may look fairly academic, but his interests are essentially practical. His reason for envying academics is that it is a profession where the culture is one that encourages the finding of thinking time above all else – it is a profession where people are paid to think.

Now in the EOB he is relieved to find that he at last does have more thinking time. But it has not always been thus. Looking back at his time running orchestras he reflects that too much time was spent 'fire-fighting' and this meant that he was seldom as effective as a leader as he would have liked to be. In running orchestras, the CEO, the Musical Director and the musicians were too often driven by the demands of the immediate future. After all, nothing concentrates the mind like the immediate presence of death, or having to perform! As a training consultant who designs and runs courses the author is only too familiar with that particular trap. So what form does the strategic thinking take?

In Richardson's opinion, strategic thinking is a question of having the time to devise the right questions. A strategy has to be formulated and the formulation has to spring from the leader's ability to ask a number of searching questions. At the EOB he considers that he is being paid to ask one essential question – 'What do we want the EOB to be in five years?'. He considers that organizations should sort out what it is they want from their leaders, and that leaders at every level should be demanding the time to think strategically. If a leader is employed for just one thing it should be to ask the demanding question and then to think ahead to form the vision that will drive the strategy. If you do not have the vision and do not spend time devising and refining the strategy, how can you offer leadership at other levels? You simply become a functionary.

So Richardson is devoting a substantial proportion of his time to the job of thinking ahead and refining the strategy. He is less concerned with the various techniques and methods available to help the leader think strategically than with the fact that he is actually doing so. When, in previous jobs, he was driven by events, he felt less content, less effective. Now that the time *is* there he feels able to look to the future more confidently.

Coping with stress

Richardson is a leader who has had his fair share of stress. Some of it was due to the amount of work that was required to lead an orchestra in what was often a difficult cultural and financial environment. More often, the stress was caused by the demands and dilemmas of attempting to lead in politically fraught circumstances where working hard to persuade others or to generate trust was simply not enough. So what has he learned about beating the old enemy?

In the past, he reflects that he has often got by through putting his head down and just working harder. In retrospect, he concludes that this was not always wise, and now he has learned to switch off at the end of the day. He concludes that throwing extra time at a problem can be the answer, but not always. The problem for the leader, however, is that it is vital to cope with stress, and it is necessary, if only for your staff, to be the same person externally no matter what is going on inside.

For Richardson, it is important that the leader shows consistency, as in his opinion, unpredictability is a sure sign of stress. The leader must be sure of his or her values and approach and, when under pressure, emphasize them with greater urgency.

Another way in which the leader can beat stress is by keeping home and work life in balance. Here Richardson considers that he has been generally successful. His wife, Janet Hilton, is a professional musician, and the couple have always shared domestic and parental duties equally. This policy has worked for both of them, and Richardson has learned to relax by doing domestic duties. He does concede, however, that there has never been enough time for relaxation or the domestic side of life.

At present, the Richardson home base is in Manchester, but David works in London during the week and commutes home at the weekend. This can lead to amusing if fraught situations. On one occasion, David met Janet at the Hilton Park motorway service station on the M6. The meeting was not intentional and they were both pleased but surprised to meet each other: he was travelling north and she was going south. Unfortunately, they were both in such a hurry that they did not even have time for a cup of coffee together. So, perhaps Richardson (or should I say the *Richardsons*) do not have the stress/time/activity conundrum licked. On the other hand, how successful in reality are the other leaders in this book?

Summary and conclusions

David Richardson comes across as a sensitive, intelligent and caring leader. He might be described as a mild-mannered man and this is meant as a compliment. However, under the sensitive exterior there burns an intense desire to succeed.

As an individual who has come to a position of leadership through artistry, and what could be defined as a greater involvement in and love of the product than you are likely to find in most leaders, there is the eternal conflict between the desire to lead and the desire to be involved. However, given the choice I would now bet with confidence that the leader would win over the musician if put to the test. The key to this conclusion lies in a revealing statement made by David Richardson, musician and leader: 'I have always moved jobs because I felt that I had done the greater part of what I could do in that situation and that there were greater challenges to meet and changes to implement elsewhere'. The leader as a change agent lives on.

Key strengths and portable quantities

- Balances competing demands of the situation to attain a set of coordinated aims.
- Sorts out his sphere of influence and establishes the best approach.

- Develops the 'reactive vision' to overcome problems and set new directions.
- Sets out to represent the organization actively to stakeholders and the overall market-place.
- Finds time to ask the demanding questions that give birth to sound strategies.

CHAPTER 9

Nancy Higgerson and Chris Grubby
Contrasts from the American South

Introduction

Both the leaders in this chapter were interviewed while I was seconded from Sundridge Park to the Center for Creative Leadership (CCL), which has its headquarters at Greensboro in North Carolina.

While I was there, I had the opportunity to talk to a large number of people about the subject, and it was while I was at the Center that a number of the ideas that underpin this book, and most certainly this chapter, were conceived. During a number of stimulating debates, I was motivated to reflect on the concept of whether leaders were sometimes just lucky to be in the right place at the right time. In other words, were they aided by being in tune with what the context demanded? I concluded that it is what the leader does that counts, bearing in mind the demands of the context as well as the constraints it presents.

Such is the impact of the context, the environment and the prevailing culture on the type and style of leadership that is most likely to be successful that it is worthwhile spending a little time examining Greensboro NC as the overall context for the two contrasting leaders described here.

Greensboro – the overall context

On flying into Greensboro from Washington in what is known by the locals as the 'vomit comet' – a twelve seater that often bounces in through the thundery summer skies – one could be forgiven for assuming that the city gets its name from the thousands of acres of trees, lakes and assorted vegetation that both surround and even enter the metropolis. But this is wrong: the city takes its name from Major General Nathanael Greene, who fought the British in a battle in the American War of Independence at Guilford Courthouse, around which the town has now grown. Nor should one underestimate the pride that the townspeople feel for their place in America's history: on absent-mindedly faxing my contact at CCL that my first working day there would be Monday 4 July, I received a dusty reply that I should learn the dates of US public holidays – and why!

Some 200 miles south of Washington, Greensboro is in what the locals refer to as the 'shallow south'. This does not mean that it is in any way slow or sleepy. In fact, it is quite the reverse. As part of the Piedmont triangle of developing towns, Greensboro is one of the economically fastest-growing places in the USA. *Under*employment is rife, and new houses are being built at a prodigious rate.

Part of the fascination of the city is the fact that it was born and has grown out of the efforts of individual leaders. Nathanael Greene gave it a name and a start, but since then entrepreneurs such as Moses Cone (who founded a textile empire producing all the denim for Levi Strauss), Smith Richardson (who gave the world Vicks VapoRub and then poured the revenue into CCL and a number of other institutions to be found around the area) and Joseph Bryan (an insurance giant who donated to medical research and founded the local business school) have helped to shape the city and community into what it is today. Greensboro also has its place in the struggle for equal rights, as it was in the downtown Woolworth store that black Americans first 'sat in' at a whites-only coffee bar to protest against racial discrimination.

In many ways, the city reflects the massive economic growth that it has experienced in recent years. A suburb without an 'urb' to go with it, there is little life left in the city centre. Vast shopping malls and arcades dominate the outlying areas and intertwine between the gracious, opulent suburban avenues. Being deep in the heart of the Bible belt it is full of thriving churches. In some areas there are two churches on every corner and the worst traffic jams are on a Sunday morning!

While I was based in Greensboro, I had the opportunity to interview two very different but effective leaders. They were different in so far that neither would have been very effective in the other person's job, given its context and demands, and it is probably true to say that neither would have felt comfortable in the other's shoes. Both, however, were actively dealing with change in large, complex organizations, and doing so in different ways. They both exhibited different approaches despite the fact that, in the final analysis, a number of common values shine through.

Put together, it is interesting to speculate on that sort of team they would make, but this is not going to happen and it is now necessary to look at each as a demonstrator of excellence in her own particular context.

Nancy Higgerson

On arrival in North Carolina, my family and I rapidly made firm friends with our next door neighbours, Liz and Paul Green, in the condominium which was to be our home for the summer. Many such condos existed to house Greensboro's burgeoning population.

Both Liz and Paul were nurses. Paul had recently taken up the appointment of Director of Nursing at the Moses Cone hostel in the city. When he heard that I was looking to interview 'guinea-pigs' for a book, he insisted that I should interview his new boss, Nancy Higgerson – 'without doubt, the reason for my being here'. With this commendation ringing in my ears, I set off for the hospital.

Context and background

Moses Cone is a large hospital by any standards: with 600 beds it occupies many acres to the north of the city. Serving the greater Greensboro area, it deals with some 57 000 casualty cases a year – 45% of whom pass on into the hospital for further treatment.

What seem like miles of smart freshly painted corridors, which make the hospital look like prime office accommodation, eventually come out into the nursing administration area, which is where I was introduced to Nancy Higgerson. Looking more like a business executive than a nurse, Higgerson manages to exhibit an aura of patience and competence. Aged around 50, she exudes confidence and unflappability, learned from years on the wards.

Higgerson's background, however, is one of a steady and determined climb through the ranks of both practical nursing and the academic qualifications necessary to underpin it and enable upward movement.

Having become a registered nurse she took a Bachelor of Nursing degree, which coincided with her appointment as Staff Nurse. Later, she further underpinned her credentials for managerial work by taking a

Masters in Nursing Administration. A one-year fellowship in a large hospital gave her an initial chance to back qualifications with real management experience, which led to her taking on the Director of Nursing role at hospitals in both Phoenix and Minneapolis. She devoted a total of 17 years to consolidating her experience at these hospitals before the offer to join Moses Cone as Vice-President, Nursing, hit her desk.

At the time of the interview she had been in her current position for five years, and still saw a challenge that would keep her in it for the long term. By any standards, her job is big in scope, both as a manager and as a leader. A total of nine nursing directors report to her, and through them she is responsible for all nursing activity throughout the hospital. As such, she walks the tightrope of representing her function to the outside world and to the medical consultants. What were the most significant lessons from her past experience that she was able to apply to her current role?

In reflecting on this question, Higgerson's calm exterior belies the determination of her words. Changes have been hitting the medical profession just as hard as elsewhere. She quickly learned that leadership and management were two very different things. In fact, the hospital environment was an ideal one for driving home this particular lesson because of the strongly competing demands of pure administration versus the more immediate demands placed on individuals by the casualty area, the wards and intensive care.

Early on, Higgerson found it crucial to find the leadership potential in other people and to foster it. 'You need to sort out the hierarchy of the decision-making process', she states, 'those decisions which should be yours alone and those which are not. You need to consider those decisions that you can give away – and feel good about doing so!'

In reflecting on the changes that she has experienced during her years in nursing she exhibits firm opinions not only on the role of the leader as change agent but also on the need for other people to support the initiatives. 'Change is difficult for everyone', she concludes, 'many more people consider it to represent threat rather than opportunity, but those who finally won't change need to step out of the way.' Higgerson is, however, far more compassionate than these words imply, as she concludes that a major part of the leader's job in managing change is to help people affected by it to move or to fit in better elsewhere. She considers that the world is changing in so many ways, and the range of talents required of people to make an effective contribution is now different.

Looking back on both struggles and achievements she comes down heavily in favour of the 'new broom' approach. 'It is a distinct advantage not having a past history with an organization when you need to be a change agent!'

Objectives and challenges

Nancy Higgerson's objectives are very clear. Stated simply, they are 'to provide the best patient care as efficiently as possible'. It is only when this statement is challenged that links to a broader vision, involving concepts of total quality, customer service and challenge to the *status quo* become apparent.

The concept of 'best patient care' to her means that patients will, irrespective of their medical conditions, be satisfied with the treatment they are receiving and will *understand* their condition. She firmly believes that this understanding will empower them and help them lead their lives, or what is left of them, as well as possible. This objective can only be achieved through the efforts of a talented and competent staff, so she is brought back to commenting about her role as teacher and developer again.

Higgerson is also clear about the main challenges facing her in attempting to achieve her stated objectives, and lists them as follows:

- To blur the lines between the different professions working at Moses Cone and to build a team that transcends hierarchy.
- To achieve this by changing the mind sets of people at all levels. A 'surgeons versus nurses' mentality too often prevails, and she sees a crucial need for the different hierarchical teams to be brought together so that differences can be lessened in the face of the common vision.
- The growth of automation in the hospital and the concurrent increase in the level of information that everybody needs to assimilate provides her with fresh challenges in working out how to develop teams that are capable of managing an area of work effectively. She considers that a lack of confidence in data management forces people into staying with the tried and tested. A major challenge for her is to get people both feeling and acting 'unboxed'.

Finally, underpinning the earlier challenges is the overarching challenge of influencing others – both her bosses as well as her staff – about the need to change attitudes, to grow and to develop.

Hints of Nancy Higgerson's overall vision for the future of nursing within Moses Cone have already been given, and when challenged to state it more clearly she is unequivocal.

The vision

Higgerson has had a clear vision for the function from the start. This was that nursing would enter the management of the hospital, both professionally and fiscally. The vision would be achieved when people at all levels *wanted* nursing to be involved in key decisions and actively sought its involvement.

This vision was not created solely by Higgerson, although the main focus of it was hers. She felt that it was vital that her management group bought into the idea, and consequently devised a committee structure to thrash out the details.

The pursuit of the vision, however, was proving to be harder. While it was easy and enjoyable to debate issues in committee, it was harder to get challenging ideas shared at all levels. To have nursing totally integrated into the management of the hospital, it was necessary to start teaching her staff what management was all about – the fundamentals of management. Paradoxically, while some elements of management were easily taught and shared, the *leadership* side of people's jobs was harder to instil. 'How do we help people to learn to lead their work units, and in doing so become more part of the overall hospital management structure?'

At the time of the interview, Higgerson was still struggling with the question of how to get the professional nurse at the bedside more in line with the vision. She concluded that while it was possible to hire new people who shared her values, there was an ongoing challenge for her with existing staff.

On reflection, she felt that it was her job to both inspire and support her staff. She did not have a single strategy for making the vision happen, but was concerned that people should share her values as a starting point, and was prepared to invest time in communicating them. If she could not easily find people who shared her values, she was more than ready to 'walk the talk' by demonstrating them at every opportunity.

In analysing and tackling the problems that might stand in the way of achieving the vision, Higgerson valued her sense of intuition, despite her logical and methodical training.

Complaints were a major stumbling block to the attainment of the vision. In dealing with them, she preferred not to react immediately, but only to do so if she sensed that a pattern was emerging. On the other hand, the intuitive antenna needed to be out all the time – 'one complaint may be nothing, but you can sometimes sense the need to intervene'.

Her sense of intuition is also needed in handling organizational politics, of which there is a great deal. Although the overall management team of the hospital has become more integrated, her office is well separated from those of other team members, so she often has to go out of her way to communicate and to pick up the latest word.

One area where power and politics come most to the fore is in her dealings with the hospital consultants. This taxes her ability to communicate and to represent her function to the hilt. Major perception gaps still exist in consultants' eyes about the role that nursing has to play. In fighting battles here, she feels that her role remains educative, although she is often dealing with long-held convictions or prejudices. What is evident is that she is a trail-blazer in fighting such battles, and here her educative approach may well prove to be more effective in the end than a purely confrontational one.

When fighting political battles, she remains convinced that mutual respect is fundamental and needs to be maintained at all costs. In achieving this respect communication is vital, as it narrows the areas of potential misunderstanding. Of course, there are political realities. Communication was easier for her to achieve between two nursing departments that required further integration, as she was able to ensure that group members met in new settings other than the hospital to deal with live issues. In dealing with them she was also able to introduce a 'little play' to help break down barriers.

While acknowledging that this approach has not been possible with the consultants, Higgerson remains determined to continue with the representational role and to be as flexible in her approach as possible.

Higgerson's vision for the future of nursing in the Hospital is also caught up with her views on the future nature of her job. Her role is broadening in terms of the number of clinical disciplines that will soon report to her, and Moses Cone itself will look very different in 10 years' time as a tidal wave of change, both technological and organizational, is on its way and needs to be caught and ridden. She sees her role, her vision, as preparing her function to ride and benefit from that wave!

Integrity and change

It is in the whole question of introducing change that Higgerson's integrity is most put to the test. It is always necessary to second-guess people's reactions to decisions and to guess what their decisions might have been in these circumstances, she reckons.

As far as she is concerned, consistency is the key. She works on the principle that people will give you trust until you demonstrate to them that you are not worth it. The old premise of treating people in the way that you yourself would wish to be treated holds true in her case, as she thinks it important not to look to blame people but to demonstrate her consistency of approach by listening hard to what they have to say and then being candid in response. Being candid is similar to being tough, but different. As far as Higgerson is concerned, it is about being 'upfront' with people: being straight, having no hidden agendas and not withholding information – even when the message may be unpopular. By behaving in this way, the essential trust remains – despite the probable outcome.

Higgerson gives an example of this approach when she had to change a premium pay plan. The changes affected approximately 80 staff reporting to her, most of whom lost out from the changes and were angry. Faced with these circumstances it would have been all too easy to get defensive or evasive, but in fact she admitted that it was a takeaway and explained the thinking behind it. At the same time, she was totally candid, stating that it was not negotiable, but also making it quite clear that she was prepared to live with the brickbats and to carry the can for her decisions.

By accepting the fact that she was the first line of defence and sticking consistently to her message, Higgerson was able to implement the changes and make them stick. This approach sums up her attitude towards empowerment. While she is sceptical about whether everybody actually wants to be empowered, she is adamant that people must be accountable and face up to their accountabilities. If they want to feel empowered at the same time – that's fine, but there can be no empowerment unless accountabilities are faced and tackled.

The facilitative approach

In getting groups and individuals to face up to their accountabilities, Higgerson states that there is a defined role of a nurse leader at Moses Cone whose function is to move groups ahead. This person will have been trained as a facilitator and the job is seen as a key role in a team-based society, as people do not always know how to work effectively in teams.

As a senior individual, Higgerson increasingly sees herself as becoming a *facilitator of facilitators* or, as she puts it, 'helping people to help other people to cope with change' as well as helping them to recognize the ongoing demands that the change will place on them.

In discussing facilitation, Higgerson is quite clear that, to her, it is different from both coaching and monitoring. It is a *call to action*, as, no matter what level of staff are involved, it is a process that is facilitated, and as a result of the process something must happen.

In using a facilitative approach, Higgerson is, in fact, deploying power, and has some definitive statements to make about this phenomenon. 'Being senior and powerful in an organization has its upside: you are heard and become part of the decision-making process; it can help you influence.' In fact, the classic music hall image of a senior nurse is of a powerful, autocratic figure, but in reality Higgerson is wary about power. She is ever-mindful of the obligations of power, preferring to define the obligations in terms of her accountabilities. She considers that power should not be exercised at the expense of others and that it is a great mistake to overtly enjoy power. In summary, she reflects that power can be tiring!

Thinker and strategist

When it comes to blue-sky thinking and long-term planning, Higgerson accepts that she is probably stronger as a facilitator and process manager. While she is open-minded about views other than her own and accepts that for every rule or policy there will be an exception, she admits that she is not a good 'far out person', finding it hard to operate much beyond a six- to twelve-month horizon. However, when she does plan she takes the trouble to ensure that she understands the overall context of the situation, and will deliberately network with colleagues at all levels to ensure her understanding.

Once the strategy begins to emerge, Higgerson communicates it energetically, paying particular attention to the most senior stakeholders, the

Hospital Director Group, consulting its members and asking them whether the strategy makes sense.

Handling stress and leisure

In any job there are times when things go wrong, and Higgerson is not too proud to look for someone with whom to talk it through. When it comes to dealing with her own stress by herself, Higgerson has a fairly simple approach: she reads novels, shuts out the world and escapes. If she needs to expend energy, she goes line dancing – the country and western-based dancing that looks deceptively simple until you try to do it. At the same time she does not think she does a good job in balancing work and non-work life, allowing work to intrude in too many ways. Attempts at adopting classic time management techniques (such as building in clear time on Fridays) work, but only to an extent!

When others are stressed, once again the facilitator in Higgerson re-emerges. In hospital life, nurses can become stressed over a variety of issues, not all of them by any means connected to the tragic elements of life in a hospital. Many are connected to workload, and Higgerson sees part of her job as helping others to say 'no'. If people are failing, she helps people to work it out for themselves by asking questions and giving feedback. When she notices a clear pattern in the failure, however, she is more directive and less likely to facilitate.

Interim comments and conclusions

So, what is it about Nancy Higgerson that makes her a good leader and what can she uniquely teach us about leadership? What competencies does she demonstrate and what are the potential downsides to someone exhibiting her style?

One of the most important things about Higgerson is that she is in many ways a trail-blazer for her profession, ensuring that her job is recognized as the senior executive position it in fact is. This very fact means that she is likely to come into conflict with other professionals who regard themselves as superior in status in the hospital and that she will have to hold her own. She recognizes that the status of her position has had to be earned, and consequently her understanding of the leadership role in her job is broad.

In pursuing her vision for the future Higgerson usually adopts a facilitative approach, even when she is in conflict with others, preferring to think in terms of helping them to see her viewpoint rather than seeking head-on collision. She is adept in so far as she is able to balance the dilemma of being a change agent with that of presenting an image of consistency by simply ignoring that there is a dilemma here.

That she engenders loyalty there is no doubt. Paul Green states that she, and the fact that she is going to be in place for a long time to come, are the main reasons for his being at Moses Cone. At the same time, nobody is perfect, and Higgerson falls into the age-old trap of being over-busy, of not allowing herself enough time to plan or think strategically. This is a pity, as she does devote a considerable amount of energy to thinking about her individual leadership role. In the end, the Achilles' heel to this accomplished leader may lie in her time management and in the prioritization as to where she devotes her 'thinking energies'.

Chris Grubby – a contrast of style and approach

If ever there was living proof of the saying that there is more than one way to skin a cat, it comes in the shape of Chris Grubby (pronounced 'Groobie').

The location for this interview was AT&T Advanced Technologies Systems, Greensboro, which is housed in enormous office blocks containing packed open-plan offices the size of aircraft hangars. These are situated some eight miles from the centre of the city and approached from peaceful country roads lined with white-painted clapboard houses and the occasional colonial style Baptist church. Although the offices stand close to a new freeway, the architects have endeavoured to create an atmosphere of calm by building a series of small lakes to break the monotony of the acres of staff car parks necessary to cater for the original workforce of 5000.

Chris Grubby is General Manager, Customer Manufacturing Services (CMS), and her role is new to the organization in so far that it exists to provide a marketing, sales and strategic planning of manufacturing service to non-defence-based electronic industry organizations. For a division of AT&T that has existed solely to provide high-tech defence systems for the US Government and its agencies, this is quite a departure. There was considerable opposition in the organization to a branching-out of this nature, and it required a dynamo to drive it and grow it. In Chris Grubby it found that dynamo!

Background and context

Grubby is a woman in what is still traditionally regarded as a man's world. In her early forties, she is small – about five foot four – and vibrant. The first impression that she gives is of energy and a friendly impatience: it is as if things just cannot happen fast enough for her. She talks fast and exudes enthusiasm with her subject matter, occasionally becoming quite carried away, her eyes sparkling with fire and enthusiasm. As she herself puts it, she *has to feel enthusiastic*, otherwise she quickly becomes bored and loses the sense of challenge that is so important to her personally.

The impatience and driving need for challenge is reflected in Grubby's past career. Her role in AT&T represents her third career change, as working life started in the teaching profession. But this was not challenging enough for her, and she was willingly seduced into the world of selling, joining Honeywell's minorities training programme and proving so successful in the selling role that she was soon promoted into management, being added to the company's high-talent list.

This listing led to Grubby being made Branch Manager of the Chicago branch, which was regarded as 'sick'. It took a couple of years to turn the branch around from being a failure to being one of the top four performing branches in the USA. These years taught her the value of energy and determination, but also how much more there was to learn about business.

A relationship brought her down to Greensboro, and although it did not result in the anticipated marriage, she decided to stay and seized the opportunity of broadening her business education with an MBA at the Bryan School of Business, University of North Carolina, Greensboro. During her time at UNCG she impressed the Dean, who helped her get in to AT&T: the third career change, as she now became involved in manufacturing operations. Now, three years on, she has helped build Customer Manufacturing Services into a $150 million operation. Reporting to Grubby are five managers, who are assisted by another 12 backup staff and approximately 80 representatives. More significantly, a further 800 people, producing the goods and services that she provides to clients, rely on her efforts to support their jobs. As such, she has to liaise with and influence factory units in Little Rock, Singapore and Europe, as well as in Greensboro.

When asked what the main lessons were from her previous experience that she has been able to apply at Greensboro, she cites a knowledge of the value of diversity as a major benefit. AT&T at Greensboro had been a male-dominated engineering-based culture that had prided itself in growing its own talent, not usually valuing outsiders as having an immediate contribution to make, and as with so many organizations that have dealt exclusively with governments, not having a strong customer focus in the way that it did business.

As a new female manager, Grubby, both in what she was and in what she did, immediately bucked the trend. Business life in Chicago had taught her the value of focusing on the customer's needs and of bringing intuition and sensitivity to negotiations, both external and internal. Central to this sensitivity was her ability to listen. The fact that Grubby had always been something different, 'the other', had taught her to accept that there would always be a diversity of views on how things should be done, and that this diversity should be welcomed, not feared. If it was possible to look at problems with a positive mind set, albeit a different one, then they could be more easily tackled in a way that addressed all parts of the issue rather than just focusing on the most obvious aspects.

Another key talent with which Grubby has learned to live is that of patience. She accepts that she is a driven person, and that the hardest thing for her is to allow others to make decisions – especially when they are not the decisions that she would necessarily have made. Letting them make mistakes and then having to spend time counselling them afterwards certainly goes against the grain.

Current challenge

For Grubby, the prime challenge is that of achieving her vision and of influencing others to help her achieve it. The significant others include individuals such as the financial manager, who needs to be updated about the impact of certain organizational procedures on CMS's costs and educated as to the reasons why she needs certain bits of financial information in order to negotiate contract pricing effectively.

To help her be more influential at a business level, Grubby set up a New Business Council, made up of plant managers and Financial Officers, to assist with reviews of the business projects on which she is working. In both individual and group contexts she is convinced of the power of internal selling. Influence for her is not constrained to the meeting itself: people must be lobbied both before and after in order to achieve the desired result.

But what of the vision itself? What is Grubby aiming at?

The vision, which Grubby wrote herself, was for CMS to be a recognized role model within the electronics manufacturing services industry, giving satisfaction both to its customers and to the people that worked for it.

Interestingly, both Grubby and her boss, the Vice-President, had visions of the future, but the VP's vision was essentially concerned with manufacturing excellence, so Grubby had to push for her view of the future. Essentially, this pushing came in the form of trying to educate the VP and others about her *outsider's* view of the future – a future in which the customer was king. This process took some time, as people had to learn to trust that this was the right way to go.

Teaching trust was in itself a challenge. Grubby saw her own role as being primarily a *champion* of the vision. Being a champion meant that she set out to benchmark and celebrate every small success on the road towards it. In talking about the vision, Chris Grubby becomes quite passionate. The vision is *her vision*: she wrote it and she desperately wants it to happen. 'If the people in CMS are satisfied', she states, 'then it follows that the customer will soon be satisfied as well. There are only five or so main customers, so this should not be difficult!' A major driver for Grubby is to lead an organization that is recognized as the 'benchmark' number one.

Overcoming fear

The vision in which Chris Grubby so passionately believes must be set against a background of fear and distrust within the organization. Over the years, change in US defence policy had resulted in a staff reduction from over 4000 to approximately 1000, with all the post-downsizing traumas that one would expect. Although the need to move out of a strictly defence-based business was generally recognized, many saw the implicit threats of doing so rather than the opportunities. The goal may have been lofty, but for many it was too lofty, too different.

For Grubby, the means to realizing the vision was through the team, and she worked with her teams to get them on its side. Although the vision never stopped being *her* vision, she would volunteer for the 'cheerleader' role within teams and fought for the airtime to put over her views. For Grubby, it was basically a question of throwing her energy and her passion at the problem. It was these not inconsiderable forces that would inspire.

Of course, there was opposition, and internal politics was involved. Where the source of the opposition was recognizable, Grubby believed in the power of one-to-one persuasion and argued energetically. However, where the source was harder to define she adopted a policy of influencing others to fight her battles for her. How? Well, in any situation there are the 'middle men' – the unaligned – and she set out to convince these floating voters, to make them to passionate about her views so that they would themselves convince the doubters.

By and large this policy worked, although Grubby herself recognizes that she tends more towards being an inspirational leader than a supportive one. Sometimes she has to force herself to listen to the concerns and worries of others rather than dismiss them out of hand. Nevertheless, she still believes that it is the leader's job to inspire people to move beyond their fear, and that consequently listening can only be a part of the equation.

Views of the future

As one might expect in someone who primarily acts as a change agent, Chris Grubby has definite opinions about the future nature of work, and although not revolutionary in themselves they are strongly held.

Managers *must* be computer-literate, she states, and must know how to handle the volume of data that they will generate. With amusement she recollects past years at Honeywell, when the organization did not allow its managers to use computers and so they did so covertly, thereby proliferating a host of different systems and approaches that further militated against efficiency.

Future demands on managers will not be to use computers – that is taken for granted – but to use the information correctly. This means not reacting to every potential trend or blip, but using them to develop well-thought out plans that will benefit the business in the long term. She anticipates that high levels of information will make managers' jobs much more challenging than they are today. There will simply be no excuse for ignorance.

A current retrogressive trend brought about by the growth in technology, she declares, is the tendency towards 'monkey management' via email and voice mail. It is all too easy to dump problems on someone via these media rather than to face up to them.

As someone who is personally highly motivated, if not driven, Grubby fears for the motivation of other people. How does one motivate people in increasingly delayered organizations? Hierarchy has had the benefit of providing a challenge and of opportunity. More significantly, she is worried about the long-term effects of recessionary times on new managers. Some managers, she states, will have spent their entire managerial careers *shrinking* organizations rather than growing them. Will they be able to adjust? Will they have a false idea of what business leadership is all about?

The candid developer

When challenged by other people, Grubby accepts the disagreement and enjoys the ensuing discussion or argument. She believes in getting things on the table and on sharing views. Her personal integrity comes across strongly in the interview, and she may sometimes sacrifice tact in favour of candour.

A time when her communication skills were taxed came when she was concerned that CMS was growing too quickly and that the supporting infrastructure was not in place. In trying to slow growth down, she was accused of 'sandbagging' sales quotas, and was personally astounded that staff might have thought that she had ulterior motives in her actions. This distressed her, as she expects candour to flow in all directions but what probably happened was that, with the best intentions, she gave out mixed messages by saying 'go for growth', but, at the same time, 'don't grow too fast'.

In her interpersonal dealings, Grubby accepts that she is better at the one-to-one level than at the group level. She recognizes the importance of teams and is involved with several of them. However, she is happiest when a team is empowered in so far as everybody knows what their role is, and that with this knowledge the team is able to make its own rules when in action. She herself is at her most effective when developing individuals and helping them to be influential by acting as a coach and mentor, and she seems more confident in this role than with group facilitation.

Strategy, problems and stress

As a strategist, Grubby can work quite happily to a two-year time horizon and sees this as reflecting the demands and project life-cycles of the type of business she is in. At the same time, she is conscious of developments that may affect it over a five- to ten-year horizon, and recognizes the need for the leader to have a longer term perspective.

When it comes to dealing with the problems that may interfere with her plans she is usually quite confident. As an analyser of problems and issues she prefers to trust her intuition, in the knowledge that the organization will provide the facts and data that in the long run may support her judgement, or at least provide ammunition for a re-evaluation. However, it is when she is alone and when she allows herself to slow down that Grubby is at her most strategic.

Not being judged on the quality or speed of response liberates her to think and plan in the long term. At other times, she allows her natural confidence to drive her forward and tackle things. This momentum means that she is not overtly concerned with the dilemmas that form a key dimension of change management, although she appreciates that other people may be less confident and therefore more likely to be confused.

When it comes to handling her own stress, Grubby tends to work harder and longer, finding satisfaction in getting things off the 'to do' list. It is when things are not in place and she feels no ability to control them or to put them in place that she gets most stressed. Feeling left out also stresses her. If something is happening and she is not part of it, her immediate reaction is – why? Grubby admits a strong desire to be part of developments and to influence them, although she accepts that this is not always logical.

When Chris Grubby does fully allow herself the luxury of getting away from it all, Garbo-like she 'wants to be alone', and relishes being in the mountains, which allows her time for some introspection: 'On the other hand, I can be at my most productive and most strategic when alone'.

Interim comments and conclusions

Chris Grubby is essentially a challenging catalyst. She enjoys a challenge and is quite prepared to challenge others and then help them meet that challenge. She is totally involved, honest and committed. In many ways a leader from the front, she goes against the grain of the current trend towards the non-ego leader – no grey person here!

Other people's perceptions of Grubby are of a dynamic, volatile influencer – somebody who has a clear vision and will set out to inspire others to help her achieve it. Where she may fall down as a leader is where others do not buy into the vision or are slow to be influenced – will she have the patience to persevere and continue to support the doubters? However, the fact that Grubby is successful is beyond doubt, and that she will invest of herself to continue this success is also beyond doubt.

Grubby herself admits that where she is most at risk as a business leader is in her dislike of management. For her, management is about administration and is, *per se*, boring. When there is no vision to chase and when the job is about maintenance, keeping self-motivation levels up will be difficult. As she herself puts it: 'if I cannot passionately buy into a vision, or if it is inconsistent to me, or if my job no longer involves its pursuit, I'll get disenchanted and leave. I don't want just to be a manager!'.

Contrasts, summary and conclusions

The most striking thing about Nancy Higgerson and Chris Grubby is how effective they are, albeit in different ways and different environments. They exhibit different competencies and are dissimilar as people. Consequently, there is a strong temptation to wonder what they would be like as a team.

Perhaps one of the most absorbing messages from these two leaders is in the way that they reflect the overall environment in which they are operating. The town of Greensboro could be described as exhibiting a number of strongly held, consistent, older-style values within a rapidly growing and changing environment – a mixture of grace and pace.

By the same token, both Higgerson and Grubby seem to encapsulate these characteristics. Although both are change agents, Higgerson is the more sedate and appears to want to build the new from a firm foundation of the past: she brings a sense of steadiness, and change, with her, is likely to be evolutionary rather than revolutionary. She represents her profession, insisting that it is valued for what it does in the organization and indicating that she will stay in place to help with the problems as well as reap the rewards of the change. She believes in using facilitative techniques to help her people to help themselves, and will be there to help them monitor the process.

Grubby, on the other hand, characterizes the high-octane push for growth and expansion. She brings passion rather than consistency to the party, and represents the dynamic project approach to business rather than the long-term view.

For both, influence is the immediate key to success, and as such they represent typical leaders in middle management positions and are faced with many of the same challenges, albeit in different contexts. Higgerson tends to see influence as being achieved through education and helping people to see things differently, while Grubby tends to see it as a challenge, and throws raw energy, passion and commitment at it.

As two separate leaders, both are effective but not perfect (that really would be asking too much!), but put them together and the result could be dramatic.

Key strengths and portable qualities

- Determined climb through profession or in career moves (both).
- Willingness to represent profession to outsiders (Higgerson).
- Clear about main challenges ahead (Higgerson).
- Identify vision for function or department (both).
- Sees role as educator, even when handling conflict (Higgerson).
- Looks ahead to future impact of technology (both).
- Candid, honest and upfront, even when the message is unpopular (both).
- Facilitative – even willing to facilitate facilitators (Higgerson).
- Passionate, energetic and keen to communicate enthusiasm (Grubby).
- Sees the value of diversity (Grubby).
- Values patience even when it goes against the grain (Grubby).
- Effective individual coach and mentor (Grubby).

Role models? Lessons? Or portable skills?

CHAPTER

10

Introduction

In the opening chapter, a number of questions were posed. To what conclusions would this small yet diverse sample of effective leaders bring us? Would their thoughts, actions and comments shed new light on the subject? Would they, on the other hand, illustrate in some way or other that the nature of modern leadership was changing at those middle levels of management, where I had emphasized the main hope for the future lies? Alternatively, would they in some way show that people were leading in much the same way as they had always done and, consequently, there was nothing new under the sun?

This, however, is the field of hypotheses, and hypotheses need to be tested. No hypothesis can be tested with validity on a sample of just nine people, and, as pointed out earlier, this did not set out to be a scientific study. Nevertheless, I would argue that if nine people from different walks of life all say the same thing on certain subjects, then those opinions should be taken seriously. So, even if neither proved nor disproved, the competencies discussed here should be noted – my view is that they are here to stay.

Far more important than any erudite arguments about scientific validity or matched competencies, however, is the essential question of 'what's in it for you?': what are the transportable, portable lessons for the leader from the work and the lives of those who have featured here? To return to the earlier analogy: what skills, attitudes and talents can be distilled and bottled from the examination of Boothman, Atkins, Sood,... – and then used for your own benefit?

But first, a brief return to the competencies and the interviews that tested them.

Testing the competencies

In every case the leaders answered the same questionnaire. However, in each case the interview developed into a conversation, and although I made sure that all questions were answered, the leaders in question did not always answer them in the strict sequence of the interview, and I have reported each 'interview' very much as the conversation developed, rather than trying to force it back into the fetters of the original question sequence. Hopefully, this has meant that each interview reflects more of the personality of the leader in question, but, equally importantly, it has enabled me to reflect the relative importance that the subjects gave in answering the various questions.

The leaders were all fluent and passionate speakers (a competency?) and they tended to speak about the things that interested them most and about which they had the strongest feelings. Occasionally, one of the subjects would state quite clearly that they did not value one or other of the competencies. Here their views were quite clear, but more often they chose to speak more about some area of their lives as leaders than others. What is probable here is not that they did not value those 'unmentioned' competencies, but rather that they were keener about others and gave them higher priority in their thoughts and deeds.

In testing the competencies, I have borne my original hypothesis in mind, namely that:

- The more competencies in which a leader readily showed a strength, the more likely that person was to be considered effective as a leader.
- A shift in the nature of leadership is taking place, with modern leaders having to take on the role of facilitator for both team and individual situations.

So, looking at the interviews and their subjects as a whole, the following areas/competencies stand out:

1. Having the vision
2. Being energetic
3. Having a sense of purpose
4. Able to handle organizational politics
5. Understanding teams and facilitative in approach
6. Being intuitive
7. Tend to welcome change
8. Are communicators – and enjoy it
9. Able to handle stress
10. Ambitious
11. Integrity – considered it paramount
12. Keenly interested in their organizations
13. Want to continue learning

The main value will come from looking at those competencies in order to examine what extra light can be shed on the nature of leadership from the interviewees' thoughts and actions.

If we look at the main areas that were stressed by all the respondents, then from these we can start to build up a list of observable competencies for leaders. By the same token, if we look at the areas that some of the leaders did not excel in but which they valued – i.e. they wished they were better at them (such as political awareness) – then it could be argued that these particular areas should be added to the list of desired competencies.

This brings us to the essential question: from the examination of these individuals, can a list be drawn up of the essential competencies that incorporate the skills, attitudes, knowledge and talents required of successful leaders today? For me, the answer is an unequivocal yes! A number of competencies were postulated and subsequently endorsed by a group of people who had two thing in common:

- They were all considered to be effective leaders by their organizations and by their peers.

- They were all at the cutting edge of leadership in so far as they were not at the very top of their organizations and they had not fallen prey to the trap of remoteness.

However, while stating that there are essential leadership competencies (which by implication can be developed), I am going to resist the temptation of listing them right now, as this would, in effect, devalue the messages that follow and reduce the likelihood of any further competencies emerging after that analysis. First of all, it is important to examine what new light can be shed on the nature of what leaders actually do, or should do, via the analysis of the areas in which the interviewees either excelled or at which they wished they could perform better.

Shedding new light on leadership

In this section, those aspects of what the leaders actually did will be individually examined with a view to seeing what lessons or advice can be extracted for you. It is not the intention here to repeat the words of those interviewed, but to give additional thoughts on the subjects, as they all appear to be valid as potential competencies. Hopefully, these thoughts will help you to develop your own approach and to form a basis for further action.

The leader's vision

Many, but not all, of those interviewed believed that they had some form of vision that had formed the basis for further action. Some saw the vision in different ways, and some, when questioned further, admitted to having a vision of what they wished to achieve from which they were able to develop their strategies. Perhaps it is the very word – vision – that is the stumbling block.

The concept of having a vision may appear to be too esoteric for some tastes. For others, the word may have almost biblical or mystical overtones that do not appear to correspond with a business situation. However, in an environment where the only certainty appears to be that confusion and uncertainty will prevail and where more is demanded of people in terms of commitment and confidence (even though the very nature of what is going on around them seems set to undermine that confidence), surely something more than just a series of orders and instructions is demanded of those in charge. It is here that the vision, as such, is desperately needed. Perhaps the answer lies in redefining it, in using different words.

Perhaps the answer lies in the fact that the leader will always need to define the reality of the situation that he or she faces and then enable that reality to be understood by others. Indeed, Max Pree, CEO of Herman Miller, stated that, 'The first responsibility of a leader is to define reality. The last is to say thank you. In between, the leader is a servant'. The term often used is that the leader must give meaning to the situation. In other words, by reaching an understanding of 'where we are now', it then becomes far easier to work out 'where we want to get to' and 'how we are going to get there'.

Of course, the vision must be a far more compelling concept than simply 'where we want to get to'; it is based on the existing mission and values of the organization and must reflect them. No matter what you call it, it is the powerful element that transforms a mere manager into a leader – the waking dream. It must be communicated – and with passion, as the passion not only defines reality more clearly but also combines it with hope.

And herein lies one of the eternal dilemmas of leadership. If the vision remains the sole possession of the individual leader, it can either become 'full or sound and fury, Signifying nothing' – the breeding ground for dictatorial thinking and enforced compliance –, or it may fail to engage the hearts and minds of those at whom it is aimed, simply because it has not taken their thoughts, hopes, fears or expertise into account. Consequently, the strengths of a visionary approach may also harbour its limitations. The only visions to which an individual can really become committed (excluding a 'road to Damascus' experience) are those that take account of that individual's values, knowledge and aspirations.

So, there is a challenge for leaders and the teams of individuals that they lead. A leader will be the sort of person who will want to shape visions, but the 'smart' leader will want to shape them with the aid of the team, perhaps to facilitate a meeting at which the raw material of the vision is criticized and then sculpted, honed and polished into shape. It is then that the vision will be truly shared rather than merely adopted.

Energy

If there was one thing, without exception, that all those interviewed had in common, it was energy. By this I mean that they gave of themselves, they went the extra mile. I do not simply mean that they worked long hours (although this they also did); what characterized them was that they kept working at a problem when others tired, they maintained enthusiasm when things were difficult and they did not give up easily; they came to be looked on as a source of energy by others when times were hard. In short, they always had something extra to give, and saw this as an essential feature of what they could bring to the job.

But it was more than extreme commitment to the task in hand, it was a sense of wanting to give everything that he or she had to offer, and not just to the job or the team, but to life. Perhaps George Bernard Shaw came closest to describing this attitude in *Man and Superman*, when he said:

> This is the true joy of life, the being used for a purpose recognized by yourself as a mighty one; the being a force of nature instead of a feverish selfish little clod of ailments and grievances complaining that the world will not devote itself to making you happy. I rejoice in life for its own sake. Life is no brief candle for me. It is a sort of splendid torch which I have got to hold for the moment and I want to make it burn as brightly as possible before handing it on to future generations.

This passionate and relevant message was put more simply but equally forcefully to me by an elderly lady in North Carolina. When I commented to her about her energetic approach to life, she replied: 'Honey, I want to burn out, not rust out!'.

So the leaders here appear to have answered that challenge, indeed to have grasped the nettle with both hands. For some, like Karuna Sood, there was a period of enforced waiting when the light had to be 'hidden under a bushel', but the message is: seize life with both hands, shake it and milk it for all that it is worth, and in turn let it use you for all that you are worth. In doing so, somewhere along the line you will probably find circumstances that will give you the opportunity to be a leader, and your mental approach will give you a head start.

Even if you do not become a leader you will have used the gift of life. *Carpe diem!*

A sense of purpose

Of course, it helps if the energy, the commitment to life, is harnessed in some way. Having a passion for life can lead you into the trap of being a busy fool if the forces are not channelled in a positive and constructive direction.

Whether they specifically called it a sense of purpose or referred to it in some other way, all the leaders had consciously worked out the direction in which they were heading, double checked that it was where they wanted to be going and then set out in that direction.

Purpose has been defined as 'the act of consciously applying our motivated strengths and resources to projects and people that move us and in which we believe'. Of course, if we really pursue our sense of purpose, a lot may be demanded of us, including courage. However, in defining a sense of purpose we can understand the deeper meaning behind many of the key elements of our lives, and in doing so we can begin to provide meaning for others as well as help us to direct our personal strengths towards those things that mean the most to us.

The increasing rate and complexity of change as we speed towards the millennium and beyond, with the resultant moral and ethical dilemmas that are raised, is making new demands on leaders. Having a definitive sense of purpose, based on identified personal values, will be a key competency for leaders, and will be a skill or approach to life and work that must be developed. I will return to how to develop a sense of purpose in Chapter 11.

An ability to continue learning

All the leaders that I spoke to had faced a variety of changes in their lives. These had often come in the form of voluntary job moves, which had placed their own demands on them, but they had also often come via technological changes to the actual nature of the business environment in which they were operating.

A common feature was that they had all coped with the changes and had learned new skills in the process. Being a leader means that you must go on learning. Several years ago I met a senior individual who sincerely stated that he considered that the fact that he was the boss meant that he did not have to learn the new skills that those more junior were struggling to obtain. What a slippery slope! But where do you draw the line?

Effective leaders need to develop an acute inquisitiveness in all developments, whether they be of technology, of market trends or of working practices – and in everything else. The knowledge resulting from the inquisitiveness helps develop an opinion, and if the opinion is valid and clearly expressed it helps confirm your position as a leader.

Then, of course, there is the whole area of mistakes. All of those interviewed had made mistakes – after all, they were not perfect! What they did possess was the ability to see where they had gone wrong and the determination not to fall into the trap again. One was particularly sanguine. 'I'm not just interested in learning from my own mistakes, but also from the mistakes I see other people make. After all, life is just not long enough to enable me to make them all myself'.

Finally, there is the role of the mentor. Several of those interviewed acknowledged the help of a more senior manager who had acted as both a sponsor and mentor. This may be an underrated element in people's progress up the organization. It is also a role that aspiring leaders should consider adopting themselves – as a crucial step in their own development.

Able to handle organizational politics

This competency has the dubious honour of not only being one that is a necessity, but also one with which some interviewees had experienced difficulty. Organizational politics, of course, has been with us since organizations began, and a long time before Machiavelli. However, with the flattening of hierarchical structures, it would appear that new and keener demands are being made on leaders to be successful political animals. So it becomes necessary to balance an ability to operate within a political environment with the necessity of operating strictly within your own sense of integrity. I will pick up this theme again later.

Understand teams and know how to use them

All the leaders valued the teams that worked for them and with them. The concept of teamwork has been one that has attracted a great deal of attention in the last few years. This attention has been generated by changes in the shape, format and hierarchical structures of organizations, and it is not the intention here to reiterate the benefits of team consensus and the resulting synergy.

What is significant was that none of the interviewees felt that they could be effective without bringing their teams with them. The question lies in the way that the leader worked with the team. If the methods of command and control usually associated with a hierarchical master/servant approach are considered to be less often appropriate, then the question stands as to what methods of leader/team working are now the keys to future effectiveness.

The answer seems to lie in the fact that the leaders in question felt that it was their responsibility to help the teams with which they were involved. To put it crudely – they recognized the need to help the teams to help them! This help could be directed at helping the teams to find the information required to progress a situation or at helping the team to address problems or even initiate strategies. The essential fact seems to be that we have a cooperative, mutually dependent process; leaders cannot do everything themselves, but they can facilitate processes with their teams that will help everybody to achieve results. Furthermore, in doing this the objectives will not simply be those of the leader, but will come to be owned by the entire team itself.

Facilitative in approach

Herein lies the key.

The scene was the bar of a large management training institution just outside Stockholm. The event was a meeting of management trainers from all over Europe, and we had come to the end of a busy day discussing further trends in our profession. There had been some tension between those who favoured an academic approach and those of us who felt that all development should be strictly pragmatic, concentrating on the potential results for the individual in his or her place of work.

After the day's work was over we had dinner on a boat that cruised the Stockholm archipelago and then, already somewhat mellow, we adjourned to the bar. A heady mixture of schnapps and beer soon revived dormant arguments, and the conversation eventually drifted on to the nature of leadership. Not surprisingly, we all had our own views on the subject and pushed them forward. Eventually, one of my colleagues put down his glass and said with emphasis, 'If you want a model for leadership, look at what we do – what are we? Well, we are the people who help others achieve things that they would never have thought possible. We help people reach conclusions, we unlock their creativity when its needed and we enable them to bring about results. Why do we do it? Perhaps we do it because we are not the conventional sort of leader that you find in today's organizations, but we are people who are acting in a way that is ahead of its time. We seldom call what we do 'lecturing' or 'instructing' – we are facilitators, and we are the unappreciated models for tomorrow's leaders'.

I was very impressed by what my colleague had said and wrote it down immediately. Soon after that the evening ended, and the following day I congratulated my colleague on his views, but found he had no recollection of the statement. I was thankful to have had the pencil to hand, as the views expressed had summed up admirably what I now consider to be the main drift of leadership activity, and an approach that reconciles the tension between the cult of the individual leader and the team-based leader. *In vino veritas!* The theme will be further expressed in the final chapter.

Being intuitive

Although the very concept of intuition can mean different things to different people, all of those I spoke to valued the use of what has sometimes been described as short-circuited logic. Some looked at the facts of a situation and then tried to intuit what lay behind them, while others were far keener to rely on what they might call their 'gut feelings'.

If we accept the concept of Brain Dominance put forward by Ned Herman and others – namely that different people will think in completely different ways and that these thought processes will be governed by the actual physical part of the brain that the individual favours, in the same way that some of us are right-handed and others left-handed, and that the part of the brain used will govern our preferred responses to certain stimuli, then it follows that different people may intuit differently.

What does come across is that all the leaders had thought deeply about their roles and approaches as leaders. Arguably, this thinking had led to insight, and this insight had formed the basis for further intuitive connection-making. So, whatever it was that was happening inside the leaders' heads, the concept that we like to call intuition was valued. It is something that can be cultivated, but like most things it needs to be given the time and attention to enable satisfactory growth.

Tend to welcome change

Alvin Toffler, in the 1970s classic *Future Shock*, made the point that everything, whether great or small, is simply a process. Every organism is a process in so far as it grows, matures, decays and disappears. So are seemingly more permanent entities, such as rocks and stones: they are all going through the process, albeit at a far slower pace. So everything is changing, and effective leaders appear to instinctively realize this fact and, indeed, welcome it.

There is, however, a far greater a challenge than that of simply holding positive attitudes towards change; a key talent for leaders has always been to make change happen. Formerly, the job was different; command and control styles prevailed in business, education and most other theatres of life, and with a general acceptance of this approach the choice of style to be used came more easily. With the social turmoil of the 1960s came a re-evaluation of many methods and ethics, including, among many people, a rebellion against authority and a demand for a different approach.

Come mothers and fathers all over this land
And don't criticize what you can't understand
Your sons and your daughters are beyond your command
Your old role is rapidly aging
Please get out of the new one if you can't lend a hand
For the times they are a-changing

For me and for many of my generation, this clarion cry from Bob Dylan epitomized the dramatic change from compliance to rebellion and paved the way for many more changes – some good, some not so good. Toffler has stated that if you were to draw a graph to represent the impact of change over the centuries it would steadily rise until the 20th century and then rise dramatically so as to become almost vertical. The 1960s shifted the line a few extra degrees towards the vertical, and now it is claimed that the final 15 years of this century will have incorporated as many changes as the previous 85 – we are truly surfing at the edge of chaos!

However, it is at this edge that both true leadership and true creativity lie.

It will never be possible for leaders to understand all the trends, pressures technologies and counter-reactions that the end of this century and the start of the new millennium will bring. It will, however, be both possible for, and a demanding duty on, leaders to welcome the atmosphere of high-octane change and to enable others not only to cope with it but, most importantly, to benefit from it.

Possessing an attitude that welcomes change and having a desire to help others benefit from it appear to be current key competencies of effective leaders – the need for these competencies will grow and grow. The future will demand a range of increasingly creative responses to the challenges and dilemmas that it presents. Perhaps true creativity is born out of the surf ride at the edge of chaos – it certainly was in such great artists as Mozart, Beethoven, Hendrix and Picasso – the leader's job will be to harness that individual creativity and to turn it to shaping a better future

Enjoy communicating

John Kotter, in his definition of leadership, stated that leaders should communicate their vision in such a way as to energize and inspire others. For this to happen, a certain level of skill in communication is implied. Without exception, all those that I interviewed were not only clear communicators but positively enjoyed speaking. Some, for example Nick Boothman, confessed to being shy as individuals, and those in my sample were by no means a bunch of raving extroverts. However, they had one thing in common – they were great talkers – and what is more, they enjoyed talking and positively welcomed opportunities to communicate.

At times, some of them confessed to being on 'transmit' for longer periods of time than they were on 'receive'. However, this may be better than not being able to communicate effectively in the first place. Surely the key to real communication in a leadership situation lies in having sufficient self-knowledge to realize when the transmit button is stuck in the 'on' position and then switching it off immediately, thereby activating the listening button.

Ability to handle stress

Stress existed in the work and lives of all those interviewed. Indeed, it is difficult to think of leadership roles where stress does not exist. It goes with the job; indeed, it goes with most jobs – a colleague of mine who was feeling the pace went to his doctor and asked what he could do to minimize the stress he felt in his job and life; the doctor looked at this healthy specimen and stated that he could try castration together with a pre-frontal lobotomy. On the other hand, if this did not appeal, he could eat less and take more regular exercise. The moral behind these dusty words is that we are all faced with stress and that we must develop the coping mechanisms that mean the most to us as individuals.

All of those interviewed had felt stress at some time, and all had successfully dealt with it or come through it when it peaked. If they did have a common weakness it was an inability to switch off. If a problem existed they threw time at it – their time. Consequently, they often worked excessive hours, sometimes to the detriment of family life. (I would have loved to have heard what was actually said when David Richardson met his wife at the motorway service station!) By and large they accepted that this was a problem, and they were supported by their families who accepted that they had demanding jobs. One interviewee, Karuna Sood, has since taken specific measures so free her time – she feels great about it. Her husband and children smile and wonder how long it will last.

Balancing ambition, interest and integrity

All those interviewed were ambitious, and several had come from quite ordinary backgrounds to something quite different. It would be condescending to say that they had bettered themselves, but they had set out to do something positive with their lives and occasionally had surprised themselves. Gill Fenwick stated, with a twinkle in her eye, that at times she reflected with some wonder that she had come such a long way from the south London school-leaver who went into teacher training college.

What universally characterized the leaders was this keen desire to do something with their lives, to move forward and to achieve. While they had all achieved a good standard of living, this was not the main motivator – they wanted to get ahead and they wanted to move their organizations ahead. They felt the need to achieve a vision in some cases, and being effective as leaders was the way to do this. Of course, not all leaders are personally ambitious, and many can be named who are not or were not. Nevertheless, in an organizational context achievement is usually related to advancement, and advancement to promotion; with the promotion comes the ability to get things done at a high level – leadership.

In addition, a further characteristic that all the leaders displayed was that of having an intense interest in their organizations. Before the reader is tempted to say, 'Well, they would, wouldn't they?', it should be pointed out that the nature of this interest went beyond normal company loyalty. It took the form of a full involvement in the company, interest in its past, passionate involvement in its present and often a preoccupation with its future. This meant that the leader was always occupying his or her mind with the business itself.

And then there was the question of personal integrity. This is perhaps one of the hardest areas to question, as it is hard to think of any leader admitting to not holding it dear – in effect, admitting to dishonesty. However, it is the emphasis with which the leaders answered questions touching on this area that made the point. Personal integrity meant a great deal to them. It was the yardstick by which they expected both to do and also be done by. Certainly, the fact that they tended to be both ambitious and to have an intense interest in the projects or areas that they were leading could have presented temptations to be manipulative or to twist the truth in their favour. Either the people I spoke to were the most accomplished set of liars that I have ever come across, or they genuinely held personal integrity to be a foundation stone of their leadership style and a guiding star of their leadership initiatives.

I trust that it was the latter and take heart from this conclusion.

Interim thoughts

So, looking back over the main talents or competencies that have been investigated, a number of features have emerged that largely favour the idea of competencies supporting the concept of WIST, outlined in the Chapter 1. Leadership can be broken down into a number of key competencies, and they will re-emerge in effective leaders irrespective of the context in which the leader operates or the personality of the leader him- or herself. However, even if most elements of leadership remain stable – predictable even – the concept retains its mysterious dimension. As Lord Slim said: 'Leadership is of the Spirit'.

Nevertheless, whether it be of the spirit or not, I noticed three distinct areas of approach and operation that appear to be on the increase. They are interesting because they reflect both what must already be inside the leader as well as how the leader must take on new behaviours in this brave new world in order to survive. This combination of attitudes and behaviours will be explored in the following chapter.

Thoughts on the nature of modern leadership
Key competencies for the future

CHAPTER 11

Introduction

In emphasizing the competencies that will follow, I do not set out to devalue those just described in any way. They remain, and will remain, of great importance; however, in choosing three from among them for extra attention and elaboration, I believe that three necessary talents that will increasingly come to the fore will have been highlighted. It could well be that in future years they will form a set of skills and attitudes without which leaders will be incapable of effective action. But why?

In Chapter 1, I referred to statements made by John Sherer, namely that fundamental change and chaos form the new context, and that what you used to do to compensate for change probably won't work this time – he goes on to say that one of the life-saving decisions for this context is to wake, to choose to be conscious. 'You don't get to choose whether you're going to be in the chaos or the confusion, but you do get to choose whether you're going to be conscious or unconscious as you move through it.'

It is with these provocative but uplifting words in mind that I have identified the three new key competencies for future leaders as:

- The ability to appreciate and handle organizational politics.
- Being able to facilitate people and situations.
- Developing a sense of purpose.

These competencies can be distilled into the three Ps: Purpose, Politics, Process.

They are, of course, not totally new. What is new is the fact that they are rapidly rising to the top of the leader's survival kitbag. The essential problem is that many leaders do not know this fact. Neither do they appreciate that the three Ps live in an uneasy alliance.

A sense of purpose is necessary, but too great a purpose may result in unhealthy levels of political game-playing and consequently pervert the purpose. Consequently, the key to realizing the purpose is through unlocking the process rather than indulging further in power plays, so, with apologies to St Paul, there are purpose, politics and process, but the greatest of the three is process; the problem is that many leaders do not know it!

The leader as politician – owl or fox?

Little has been written about organizational politics, either because many find the subject distasteful or perhaps because it is deemed to be unworthy of study. Neither is it found in the syllabus of any management programme or MBA course that I have come across. What a waste! It is possible that more people's careers flounder on the rocks of organizational politics than for many other reasons. Indeed, as a management trainer, a high proportion of the extra-curricular questions (i.e. those asked in the bar at the end of the day) centre on this thorny area.

So how can politics be defined and, more importantly, how can it be survived?

If company politics can be described as 'the way we do things around here', then surely it can also be described as 'the way that we do things to people around here'. It is a sad truism that wherever people gather to tackle a task there will be tensions, rivalries, jealousies, hidden agendas and plain old-fashioned mischief. Not only do people want to achieve the task their own way, they also want the way that the task is approached to reflect glory in certain specific directions and to help the careers of specific individuals or groups. It may not be pleasant, but, whether your place of work is a merchant bank or a monastery, it is unavoidable. Indeed, there is evidence to show that the more senior and better educated the participants, the more prevalent and unpleasant will be the politics. At Marks & Spencer's Head Office in London in the 1970s a number of highly qualified, talented individuals played fast and furious political games. The reason? The awesome organization in its retail stores did not extend to Head Office, where many senior professionals were somewhat underemployed. As the saying goes, 'the devil makes work for idle hands', and the spare hours were filled with all sorts of intrigue.

The concept of political animals is a popular one, and the University of Birmingham has conducted intriguing studies on the nature of these beasts in organizations. Researchers identified two axes of behaviour:

1. That of being 'well-read' in what was going on politically within the organization: having an interest in the different factions' power camps and power plays. The degree to which one was well-read could be high or low.
2. That of having an interest in self and the promotion of one's own aims versus that of having a prime interest in the fortunes and welfare of the organization.

With these axes in mind, it then became possible to identify four discrete orientations and to label each with the name of the animal most representative of that particular orientation.

- *Orientation 1* Here the individual was politically well-read and had a high interest in the fortunes of the organization rather than self. This individual they labelled the Wise Owl. Owls are both liked and respected; furthermore, they are seldom hunted and usually survive. There is one downside, however: they do not often get to be head of the forest.
- *Orientation 2* In this box the individual was well-read and took an active interest in the politics; moreover, the individual promoted him- or herself actively within the organization. Here we have the Crafty Fox. The fox is not always popular, for it hunts and it can create mayhem, but usually it is a survivor. Occasionally it oversteps the mark and is hunted down, but even then it has an excellent chance of survival (if the efforts of the fox hunt in the area of southern England where I live are anything to go by, I'm glad to say!).
- *Orientation 3* In the first of the lower boxes is found the person who is politically ill-read, but who on the other hand has a high degree of self-interest. The researchers contemptuously labelled this individual as the Donkey – both stubborn and

stupid. The donkey is used as a beast of burden, resents it and is seldom thanked. It never reaches the top.

- *Orientation 4* The final box contains those who are badly read politically, who have no interest in improving their knowledge or skills and yet who continually put the organization before self. Loyalty, blind loyalty, is the name of the game, and these people are labelled Sheep, unquestioning and naïve. It often happens that the sheep end up in the slaughterhouse.

So where is the best position to be politically? Having put this question to a wide variety of executives from different countries and cultures, the answer is invariably 'just to the right of the Fox/Owl divide (i.e. a combination of both, but being slightly more of a Fox). In other words, they were saying that you have to know the political forces at work and have to keep up to date with the trends and developments here. In addition, you have to know how to play the game in order to appreciate the 'games' that may be played against you – and to take counter-measures where appropriate. However, they were also saying that the game was not worth the sacrifice of one's own personal integrity and self-respect. So, to survive, the effective leader must be 'aware' and must learn to apply this awareness in ethical ways that reinforce the leader's credibility rather than detract from it. All the essential skills of questioning, listening and above all intuition must be used to the full. Having the antennae out at all times is not being manipulative and does not sacrifice integrity: it is simply being smart.

The leader as facilitator

If we are indeed surfing on the edge of chaos, which is where real creativity and innovation are born, then there is a need for new leadership skills that will help realize this creativity.

Those leaders who rely simply on compliance as a weapon will not be effective; neither will those who over-rely on the visionary approach, as the only visions to which individuals can become positively committed are those that take account of their personal values and aspirations. The leader can still initiate a vision, but it must be shaped by the followers, not blindly adopted – and herein lies a challenge to both leaders and teams alike.

Roger M. Schwarz, in *The Skilled Facilitator*, identifies the key differences between the normal facilitator and the facilitative leader which can help identify the key differences of approach that are required and lead on to an examination of the most effective behaviours that can be employed.

The essential differences are that:

- The facilitator is a third party, while the facilitative leader is part of the group.
- The facilitator is neutral, while the facilitative leader is deeply committed.
- The facilitator is a process expert but not a content expert, while the facilitative leader must be an expert in both process and content.
- The facilitator has no decision-making authority, while the facilitative leader does.

However, to fully understand facilitation we need to look at what it is that facilitators do.

For a start, facilitation must not simply be thought of as confined to the lecture room. Although vital to successful outcomes in management development, it is an equally vital tool in general consultancy and in creating success in meetings, albeit without authority.

Facilitation is allied to coaching and teaching, but is different. It has a more important element of leadership within it. To facilitate is to ensure the process of something, to deliver a positive outcome. What distinguishes it is that it is most often done with groups, where participants are encouraged to take responsibility for their own outcomes. The quality of the facilitation is evident in the way that the facilitative leader chooses to work with the group.

This may sound easy, but it is not. Effective facilitation makes its demands on the facilitator to become over-reliant on one simple style. The challenge to all facilitative leaders is to develop a range of styles, therefore enabling themselves to manage processes more effectively. In examining facilitation I have identified four distinct styles.

Intellectual command

This approach is characterized by a high degree of input of data, opinion and information to the group, but a comparatively low level of intervention into the way that the group members interact with each other to achieve objectives, i.e. the process. The facilitative leader's behaviour should involve guiding by having clear opinions, provoking and answering questions, setting challenges for the group and inputting facts and knowledge where deemed to be necessary.

Intellectual command is appropriate where the team has clear, task-related objectives yet may lack specialist knowledge or information. This lack may be hindering progress, and members may be hungry for knowledge or direction. In the past, the group may have become used to being told the 'right way' by a guru-style leader. It may have a lot of potential energy, but needs the challenge of informed and structured questions to release this energy.

This approach makes a number of requirements of the leader, who must be able to display an authoritative understanding of the subject matter or the objectives that the group is addressing. Those working in this mode must retain a clear mind and objectivity at all times, have clear opinions and the confidence to state them, and have the flexibility to address the problem from a number of different angles. This will enable them to phrase demanding questions and to 'wow' team members with their demonstrable insight.

Incentives approach

This approach is characterized by a high level of input to the knowledge base of the team, as well as a high level of intervention in the process of the group. Groups requiring this approach to motivate them may be characterized by an overall lack of energy or commitment, observable cynicism from some members and possible open conflict against the tasks and objectives of the group. There may be a number of 'Why are we here?' and 'What are we doing this for?' questions.

It is the responsibility here of leaders to assess the situation and then to drive the group to a more productive state and atmosphere. They must be able to focus the group, to handle any overt conflict and to draw out both the negative and the positive emotions existing within it. Fact and opinion are stated, but equally important is that the process of the group is actively influenced by strong and possibly courageous behaviour. If it is necessary to use the stick and carrot, to stress the implications of failure, then this is the time.

This approach makes different demands on facilitators. A firm knowledge base is helpful, but not enough. High energy, assertiveness and the ability to both give and receive criticism are all requirements here. It is the energy and firmness illustrated in this approach that will kick-start the group. The motivation may not be immediate, but later, when motivation is higher, members may look back on that intervention as a turning point.

The creative group catalyst

This approach is illustrated by less intervention in the group process and a low input of facts and opinions. Teams benefiting from this approach will have a desire to solve their own problems and have a high opinion of their own ability. They may, however, need some steering towards achieving their objectives and may need to be challenged in order to release further energy.

The facilitative leader's role here is hard for many people, as it involves the stimulation of the group, although not in an overt way. Actions may involve helping members to set the agenda, giving occasional feedback on the process and helping the group to explore new tasks or issues. The main task of the facilitator will be to allow the team to be more creative or productive, and this may involve the phrasing of thought-provoking questions and giving the occasional steer, but above all knowing when not to dominate. Then, having given a small steer, the leader must have sufficient self-control to step back and let the team members take control. The motivational effect of this form of behaviour lies in the fact that members will think that they have achieved everything themselves and will therefore be spurred on to attempt even greater feats. It is through the effective use of this style that creativity and innovation can most often be stimulated.

The supportive coach

Once again this is a different style, where the approach involves a comparatively low level of knowledge input but a higher level of intervention on the process of the team. Teams benefiting will be characterized by a general lack of confidence; they may be finding the task difficult or may not have a clear idea as to what to do next. Individuals within the team may be operating at different levels of confidence or ability.

Leaders in these situations will need to do a great deal of looking and listening, they will need to know when to give encouragement, when to be helpful and when to single out those in particular difficulty. They must be able to inspire trust and be willing to listen and empathize with people's feelings. They must also have the ability to promote understanding in a non-challenging way. While other approaches may well motivate the team through challenge or stimulation, this approach will achieve motivation through a process of building and growing of both group and individual confidence.

Choices for the facilitative leader

The four approaches require flexibility of approach from the facilitator as well as an ability to judge the appropriate type of intervention at both team and individual levels. It is probable, however, that there will be a tendency for teams to move towards requiring the creative group catalyst approach as they mature. The more a group of people is thus facilitated, the more it will become accustomed to drawing its own conclusions, to making its own decisions. It may be a harder group to manage, but it will produce better results. In short, it will be a credit to its leader.

General prerequisites for the would-be facilitator are a level of courage and a willingness to experiment outside your preferred styles. A level of sensitivity will also be necessary, and the ability to observe a group and to judge accurately the right approach to stimulate the best results from it will be crucial. Each style will, however, pose different development challenges for the developing facilitative leader, and the challenge will be for the leader not to act in a unidimensional manner but to be able to facilitate in at least three of the four styles.

Facilitation is about unleashing creativity, and that in itself will lead to innovation. Often conflict exists over the right approach to making innovation happen. It takes place in the midst of politics, lack of trust and unshared values. It is in the middle of this potential quagmire that the need for facilitative skills in the leader comes to the fore. In his article 'Leading with Innovation in Mind', Peter Frost acknowledged that not all innovation was good and not all opposition to it was bad. He did feel that lack of understanding of it, however, was dangerous, and stated: 'Perhaps the best hope for checks and balances in the process of innovation will be a more widely shared understanding of how the innovation process works so that all the actors and stakeholders involved in an innovation project can contribute to a workable resolution'. Bring on the facilitative leader!

A sense of purpose

Having a sense of purpose can justifiably be described as 'the act of consciously applying motivated strengths and resources to projects and people that move us and in which we believe' – a lofty, if not intimidating statement. How can this best be done?

The sense of purpose can only exist for one reason: to produce a product. And for a sense of purpose to become more than some vague longing or abstract desire it must be clarified and quantified. The process here must be one of identification of where the drive comes from. Is it from the head, in that the desires are based on calm analysis, logic and calculation, or is it from the heart, in that it is made up of a number of strong and perhaps contradictory emotions? There is little good in harbouring some generalized wish such as 'I want to make the world a better place': such wishes can only be of any use when they start to mobilize the individual.

The first step must be for you, as leader, to recognize the source of drive and ideally to engage both heart and mind in its analysis:

- How do I put it into words?
- Is what I want realistic?
- Is it ethical?
- Do I want it for selfish or for altruistic reasons?
- Is it obtainable?
- Can I articulate what it is that gets in my way and drains my energy? How can it be avoided?

If the drive stands up to this simple but vigorous scrutiny then it is most likely valid. In other words, permit the drives to crystallize your sense of purpose and start thinking about the personal development that you will need to accomplish these desires. After all, the 'drivers' of an individual make up a significant proportion of that person's personality. It is at about this stage that the personal vision is often born, and this vision should really start pressing for an answer to the question, 'What do I want to do with the sort of person that I am?'.

Further steps in the development of a true sense of purpose must be:

- To be focused in your aims while still keeping a perspective on the balance of energies devoted to both home and work.

- To remind yourself constantly of your core values and to check whether the drive is centred on them.
- To allow the knowledge of your core values to make you more confident in what you do and to allow you to demonstrate that confidence to others.
- To use your confidence to make your own decisions and to challenge others when they try to make them for you.

However, before the personal vision can be truly clarified it is necessary for the individual to plan the steps on the path of personal growth that will be trod on the journey to become worthy of the desires. After that, the dreams become valid and a source of personal motivation – hopefully a source of inspiration to individuals that will make them more able to make a valid contribution via their lives to the societies and to the organizations in which they spend their lives.

And if all of the above seems somewhat serious, if not 'driven', then, as a final thought in developing a valid sense of purpose – are you allowing yourself to have fun on the way? If not, then think again – you only live once! On a practical note, time spent in relaxation, enjoyment, laughter or creation refreshes the spirit and renews momentum. And ultimately, it reinforces the strength of purpose.

Faced with the wild gallop of change in all our lives it can only be the combination of many senses of purposes, grown into mature drives and translated into ethical, yet effective, leadership that will make us masters of the process rather than its victims. There was a time when evolution was the key word, but no longer. Combined senses of purpose can produce valid visions for a future where the revolution of change is planned, controlled and turned into something that can benefit all of mankind rather than the lucky few. If this does not happen we may all find ourselves staring into the abyss.

Conclusion

So, is it possible to define key competencies of leadership – competencies that can be bottled by the aspiring leader and used for personal development, or, better, as targets for achievement?

For me the answer to this question is a definitive *yes* – especially if the dry word 'competency' is replaced by the concept of the right attitude, the right levels of knowledge and the skill necessary to do something positive with them. Furthermore, if competencies are looked at this way they are readily replaceable by the word 'talent' – a more satisfying, descriptive and challenging concept. We all have talents and we all are challenged to do something with them.

In examining the competencies, or talents, it becomes clear that there are some things that effective leaders will always need to do and some new aspects of leadership that are already becoming of increasing importance. Once again these new things span action, knowledge and attitude, and can therefore be referred to as new talents to be developed.

Furthermore, in speaking to the variety of leaders I was increasingly struck by the lessons for others that emerged in discussions about what they did and thought at work. Samuel Butler once said, 'Every man's work, whether it be literature, or music, or pictures, or architecture, or anything else, is always a portrait of himself'. So, in looking at these portraits of working, sometimes struggling, leaders, at their thoughts and at their work, hopefully we have been looking at the core of leadership itself.

In trying to synthesize the old and new talents and in trying to paraphrase the lengthy list of competencies identified earlier, I have come up with the following top 10 tips for present and future leaders.

1. Sort out which parts of your job involve leadership as distinct from management. What talents will you need to develop to be effective?
2. Recognize that leadership is about promoting change, so embrace it for the opportunities that will occur.
3. Go out of your way to promote learning in others. Do not think of yourself as a boss, but as a facilitator.
4. Organizations must learn in order to adapt, so take every opportunity to be a learner yourself. Seek a mentor and seek to be a mentor.
5. Make time to think about your job as a leader. What demands does it place on you and how are you reacting to them?
6. Remember that leadership is about working with people and making choices as to how to approach them and how to

motivate them. Are you making the right choices and are you politically 'well-read', even if not politically motivated?

7. Increasingly you will be dealing with diversity of approach, gender, race and nationality. Welcome it, because therein lie the seeds of creativity.

8. Learn to think and act strategically. Balance the big picture with understanding of its likely impact on you and your people.

9. Leaders can decline. Often the first sign is when the vision fades. Do you have a vision? How strong is it, and is it backed by a sound sense of purpose?

10. Remember WIST. Standing for Wisdom, Integrity, Sensitivity and Tenacity, it both includes and supports all the competencies and talents required for effective leadership.

Of course, this list is a general one, and it does not attempt to specify everything that has emerged here. The reason? Leadership remains of the spirit, and thus will continue to resist attempts to over-analyse or specify it. Unlike the tools of management, which are essentially about measurement and which therefore themselves can be measured, the tools of leadership can be noted but less readily subjected to this kind of scrutiny. With this in mind, what I and those who were kind enough to contribute to this book have said about the subject should be seen as advice and as guidelines (hopefully good advice and guidelines) rather than as a prescription.

Nevertheless, if it is admitted that leaders are vital in shaping the future and optimizing the present, then surely something should be done with the identified talents that make for effective leaders. Formal courses and qualifications for management abound, but none exists purely for the promulgation of better leadership. In discussing leadership, we have inevitably focused on change so why not end on a futuristic note? Will the next decade see the decline of the Master of Business Administration and the rise of the Master of Business Leadership?

I hope so.

The portable leader questionnaire

Method

Use the questionnaire to generate a general discussion around the points raised by the following questions rather than taking too pointed or specific an approach which could potentially telegraph the desired answers rather than stimulate a spontaneous response.

The context

1. Please give me the following introductory details. Your job title. Number of direct reports and a sample of their job titles. The main purpose of your job and what you see as its main objectives.
2. Tell me something of your background before taking on your current role (e.g. education, previous employment, progress within your current organization).
3. Were there any lessons that you have learned from your previous life or work experience that you have been able to apply to your leadership role in this job?
4. Please describe the context of your current role. For example, describe the organization – its product or service – its purpose and stated objectives. What makes it special in your eyes?
5. What do you see as the main challenges of your job as a leader within the organization?
6. What type of people do you need to influence to achieve your objectives?
7. What have you achieved to date and what achievements appear within your grasp?

Competencies – W

8. When you started out on this job or assignment, what sort of picture did you have of what you wanted to achieve?
9. How did you go about pursuing this vision? Give some examples. Was this a solo exercise, or was the vision formulated in some other way?

10. What does the concept of being inspirational mean to you?
11. Please contrast the two words 'inspire' and 'support'. Can you give any examples of having acted deliberately in either mode of behaviour?
12. How did you go about tackling the problems that you experienced in attaining the vision? How in fact did you perceive them? Can you give examples? Did you use intuition? Did you use judgement? Or do you prefer to go through a process of logical analysis?
13. How do/did you know that the vision was being achieved? Can you give any examples?
14. In terms of any office politics involved, how did you perceive them? How do you think you handled the politics?
15. Have there been occasions where you have actively needed to influence others or persuade then to do something that went against the grain? Please give examples of the situations – and what you did. With position comes power. How much power do you think you have? How do you feel about it? What do you consider to be the advantages *and disadvantages* of having power?
16. Thinking ahead: how do you see the nature of your job changing in the future?
17. What do you think jobs, organizations and the work they promote will look like in 10 years' time?
18. What do you understand to be the essential differences between leadership and management?

Competencies – I

19. In your work as a leader, can you give any examples of having to demonstrate trust in others and also to demonstrate trustworthiness?
20. How do you feel about 'hidden agendas' in business life?
21. Being candid is a virtue. Does this always apply? Please give any examples from your experience.

Competencies – S (in relationships)

22. Describe a situation in which your communicative abilities were stretched. What did you do? What did you learn from the situation?

23. Tell me about your staff. What are their most common strengths and weaknesses? How are people developed? What have you done?
24. What does the word 'empowerment' mean to you? Give examples.
25. What are your views about learning in the workplace?
26. Is yours a team-based environment? What are your views on teams? What do you consider to be the future of teams in the work environment and how can they be best used?
27. What does the word 'facilitation' mean to you? Is it a concept that can be applied to leadership situations, and if so, how?

Competencies – S (in thinking)

28. How do you go about problem-solving and ideas generation?
29. Rules and procedures are there to help, or hinder – comment.
30. How do you feel about alternative views to your own being discussed or implemented?
31. What responsibility do you consider you have to shape the culture of your organization (or part of it)?
32. How much time do you devote to strategic thinking? How do you go about it? What do you take into consideration?

Competencies – T

33. How do you cope with pressure and stress?
34. When colleagues or subordinates get stressed, what do you do?
35. How do you set out to balance work and domestic life?
36. What do you do when things do wrong? Give examples.
37. What are your views about failure? Is there any upside to this phenomenon?
38. How much change is there in your work environment? How do you feel about it? What do you do about it?
39. Change may bring with it uncertainties and dilemmas. Can you give any examples that have affected you? What did you do?
40. What else would you like to add about yourself, your approach to leadership or your situation?

Bibliography

Drath, Wilfred and Palus, Charles J. (1994) *Making Common Sense*, Center for Creative Learning, Greenboro, North Carolina.

Kotter, John (1990) *A Force for Change*, Collier Macmillan, London.

van Maurik, John (1994) *Discovering the Leader in You*, McGraw-Hill, London.

van Maurik, John (1995) *Facilitating Excellence*, MCB Publications, Manchester.

MCI (1994) *Management Standards*, Crown Copyright.

Schwartz, Roger M. (1994) *The Skilled Facilitator*, Jossey-Bass, San Francisco.

Shaw, George Bernard (1903) *Man and Superman*.

Toffler, Alvin (1973) *Future Shock*, Pan Books, London.